221 GREAT EXPLORERS of the WORLD

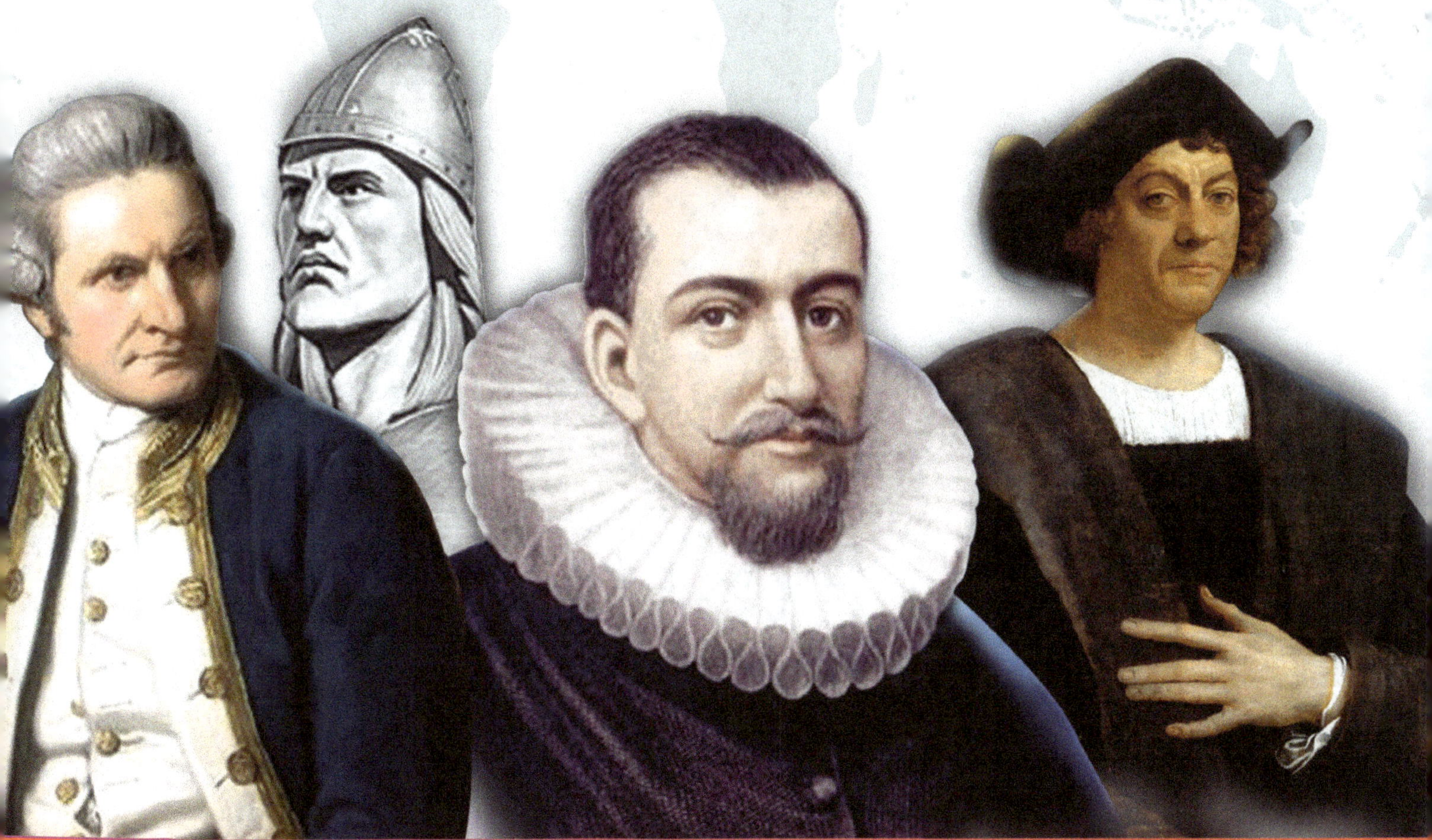

MANOJ PUBLICATIONS

221 Great Explorers of the World

Publishers:

MANOJ PUBLICATIONS

761, Main Road, Burari, Delhi-110084

Mobile : 09999476076, 9868112194, 8178823569, 8178854810

Email : info@manojpublications.com

For online shopping visit our website :
www.sawanonlinebookstore.com

ISBN : 978-93-86626-47-9

GREAT EXPLORERS OF THE WORLD

The human race has always been curious and mystifying. We have thirst for knowledge that has led us to venture beyond the known boundaries in order to find, know and discover more. Explorers have changed the face of the world as we know it and have expanded our reach to the remote corners of the Earth previously unknown or forgotten.

This book brings together the people who in various eras have set forth into realms unknown to discover new lands going beyond fear, adversity and hardships.

How do these personalities impact us?

The 'Great Explorers of the World' helps us understand how the world we know and live in was shaped, bit by bit, piece by piece. It becomes very easy to fire your curiosity and idolize these personalities when you read about the sheer grit and determination it takes to undertake such arduous voyages and come out a winner despite overwhelming circumstances.

Reading about these brave people nudges the reader to start working towards his goals and go beyond his fears and uncertainty.

Why is it important for you to read this book?

This book puts together the most noted explorers of the world for your perusal. They have made major contributions in mapping the world we live in today. These are the people who laid the foundation of civilisation all over the planet besides helping us understand the world we live in, from rivers, gorges, mountains, continents to the moon and space.

To read about them is knowledgeable, inspiring and thrilling all in one.

Can these explorers really make a difference in your life?

Yes, beyond doubt! The human mind is a sponge soaking in all that it sees and learns. Having role models and, constantly reading affirmative materials about such people impacts our minds and, hence, our life in a very positive way.

Our aspirations grow and we realise after reading about explorers that anything is possible when we are determined to pursue our dreams with hard work and dedication.

CONTENTS

1. Marco Polo

Marco Polo was born in 1254 in Venice, Italy, and he died on 8th January 1324 (aged 69-70 years) in Venice. Marco Polo was a Venetian merchant who undertook an epic journey to Asia, including India, China and Japan, and returned 24 years later. He recorded his travels in the book 'The book of Marvels' which he dictated to his fellow prisoner, Rustichello, when he was imprisoned during the Venetian war with Genoa. He was the first explorer to leave a detailed chronicle of his travels. There is dispute as to whether the Marco Polo family is of Venetian origin, as Venetian historical sources considered them to be of Dalmatian origin.

Do you know: Marco Polo's book inspired Christopher Columbus and many other explorers to visit those eastern lands.

2. Christopher Columbus

Christopher Columbus was an Italian navigator, born on 31st October 1451 in Italy and he died on 20th May 1506 (aged 55 years) in Spain. Christopher Columbus discovered the 'New World' of the Americas on an expedition while trying to find a route to India making four trips across the Atlantic Ocean from Spain between 1492 and 1502. He introduced Horses to the New World on his subsequent visit. Between 1492 and 1503, Columbus completed four round-trip voyages between Spain and the Americas.

Do you know: Christopher Columbus kept thinking that he had discovered a short cut to Asia across the Atlantic Ocean; he never realised that he had made such an important discovery.

3. Amerigo Vespucci

Amerigo Vespucci was an Italian, born on 9th March 1454 in Florence and he died on 22nd February 1512 (aged 58 years) in Seville, Spain. Amerigo Vespucci undertook several expeditions during which he discovered Brazil; he recognised that South America was an all new continent and not an extended part of Asia. After being made the Chief Navigator of Spain he established a school of navigation to standardize and modernize navigation techniques developing an almost accurate method of determining longitude.

Do you know: The name America is the feminine version of Amerigo Vespucci's Latinised name, Americus Vespucius.

4. *Vasco da Gama*

Vasco da Gama was born in about 1460 in Sines, Portugal, and he died on 24 December 1524 in Kochi, Portuguese India. In 1497, Vasco da Gama was appointed to command a ship with the goal of discovering a sailing route to India. A nobleman commissioned to find a maritime route to the East, he was successful and became the first European to sail to India around Africa allowing the Portuguese to establish a colonial empire in Asia. He fleet sailed for 23 days before landing at Calicut, India on 20 May 1498. Vasco da Gama was the second Portuguese Viceroy of India.

Do you know: On his first voyage Vasco da Gama covered 24,000 miles in two years with four ships which only 54 of 170 crew members survived.

5. *Captain Meriwether Lewis*

Captain Meriwether Lewis was born on 18th August 1774 in Virginia and he died on 11th October 1809 (aged 35 years). As the leader of the Lewis and Clark Expedition his mission was to explore Louisiana Territory. He collected scientific data on indigenous nations, the flora and fauna of the area. Captain Lewis and Clark appears on the gold dollars minted for Lewis and Clark Centennial Exposition and a 3-cent stamp on the 150th anniversary. Lewis had no formal education until he was 13 years of age, but during his time in Georgia he enhanced his skills as a hunter and outdoorsman. He became interested in natural history, which would develop into a lifelong passion.

Do you know: The state flower of Montana, a woodpecker and a river are all named after Captain Lewis.

6. *Lieutenant William Clark II*

Lieutenant William Clark II was born on 1st August 1770 in Virginia, United States, and he died on 1st September 1838 (aged 68 years) in Missouri, United States. William Clark was the other leader of the Lewis and Clark Expedition exploring the Louisiana Territory and was responsible for hiring and training men for the expedition. Later, he served as the Governor of Missouri Territory. In 1807, President Jefferson appointed Clark as the brigadier general of the militia in the Louisiana Territory.

Do you know: A plant and a bird species have been named after clark. These are the species he identified during the expedition. He appears on the gold dollars minted for the Lewis and Clark Centennial Exposition and was honoured with a 3-cent stamp on the 150th anniversary.

7. *Neil Armstrong*

Neil Alden Armstrong was born on 5th August 1930 in Ohio and he died on 25th August 2012 (aged 82 years) in Ohio, United States. Neil Armstrong was the first man to walk on the moon. He got his pilot's licence at the age of 15 and later joined the navy as a fighter pilot. He went on to become a test pilot before he applied to become an astronaut and was selected by NASA in 1962. His first trip into space was aboard the Gemini 8. On 21st July 1969 he stepped onto the moon from his spacecraft Apollo 11 and stayed on the moon for 21 hours along with another astronaut Buzz Aldrin. They collected moon rocks.

Do you know: The footprints of Neil Armstrong and Buzz Aldrin are still there on the moon as the dust is thick but there is no wind to blow it away.

8. *Ferdinand Magellan*

Ferdinand Magellan was born in 3 February 1480 in Portugal and he died on 27th April 1521 (aged 41 years) in Cebu, Philippines. Ferdinand was the first man to circumnavigate the globe. He sailed with five ships and over 270 men. They finally made it to the Mariana Islands where they stocked up on food and headed towards the Philippines. Ferdinand was killed in battle there. Only one of the five ships made it back to Spain three years after they had started with only 18 surviving sailors. The Magellanic penguin is named after him, as he was the first European to note it.

Do you know: Information about Ferdinand Magellan and the voyage is known through a journal written by a sailor Antonio Pigafetta who recorded all that had happened on the journey.

9. *Hernan Cortes*

Hernan Cortes was born in 1485 in Medellin, Spain, and he died on 2nd December 1547 (aged 62 years) Castilleja de la Cuesta, Spain. Hernan Cortes was an intelligent administrator, ruthless fighter, and capable leader. He conquered the Aztec Empire for Spain, killing the Aztec King with the help of the Tlaxcala people. When put in charge of the expedition he landed there with ships, men and cannons to take over the Aztecs. From the New World where he came at the age of nineteen, he moved to Cuba where he became wealthy and powerful. He participated in the conquest of Cuba and Hispaniola and was rewarded with Indian slaves and a large estate of land for his contribution during the expedition.

Do you know: The Gulf of California was originally called the Sea of Cortes.

10. *John Smith*

Captain John Smith was born in 6 January 1580 in Willoughby, England, and he died on 21st June 1631 (aged 51 years) in London, England. The founder of the first permanent English colony to settle in Virginia, John Smith arrived there in 1607 to set up the Jamestown colony when he was captured by the Native American tribe of Powhatan to be executed. He was buried in 1633 in the south aisle of Saint Sepulchre-without-Newgate Church, Holborn Viaduct, London. The chief's daughter, Pocahontas, saved his life. He also explored the northern coast of America and called it 'New England'.

Do you know: In 1602, John Smith was captured and sold into slavery but he managed to escape and travel all the way back to England.

11. *Francisco Pizarro*

Francisco Pizarro was born around 1471 in Spain and was assassinated on 26th June 1541 (aged 70 years) in Lima, Peru. Francisco Pizarro was a colonist who conquered the Inca Empire for the Spanish Empire by taking the Inca King Atahualpa prisoner, holding him for a ransom but killing him despite getting it. Hearing of the great wealth of Peru he had tried twice before he succeeded on his third attempt to set up the first Spanish settlement in Peru. By his marriage to N de Trujillo, Pizarro had a son also named Francisco.

Do you know: Francisco Pizarro was a pig herder before he became an explorer.

12. *Captain James Cook*

Captain James Cook was born on 7 November 1728 in Marton, England, and he was killed by Hawaiin natives on 14th February 1779 (aged 50-51 years). A British navigator and cartographer who mapped much of South Pacific, New Zealand and Australia, James Cook set off on his first voyage on 26th August 1768 to observe Planet Venus as it passed between the Earth and the Sun to help astronomers calculate the distance of the Sun from the Earth. The Australian Museum acquired Cook Collection in 1894 from the Government of New South Wales.

Do you know: The sailors on James's ship, Endeavour, got tattoos done from Maori warriors on their arms and started a tradition that continues today.

13. *John Cabot*

John Cabot was born 1450 in Genoa, Italy and he died around 1498-1501. Sailing to Canada thinking it was Asia John Cabot claimed it for Henry VII of England. Also claimed for England the east coast of North America somewhere near Labrador or New foundland in the modern day Canada. The plan had been to sail west across the Atlantic Ocean to find a shorter route to Asia. He claimed to have found land full of silk and spices. Like other Italian explorers, including Columbus, John Cabot led an expedition on commission to another European nation. In 1496, John Cabot made a voyage from Bristol with one ship, but he was forced to turn back because of a shortage of food, inclement weather, and disputes with his crew.

Do you know: John Cabot was known as Giovanni Caboto before he moved to England.

14. *Jacques Cartier*

Jacques Cartier was born on 31st December 1491 in the Duchy of Brittany and he died on 1st September 1557 (aged 66 years) in Saint Malo, France. The first European to travel inland in North America and to describe and map the Gulf of Saint Lawrence and shores of the Saint Lawrence River which he named 'The country of Canadas'. He's credited with naming Canada and claiming it for France. He opened up the greatest waterway for the European penetration of North America. He spent the rest of his life in Saint Malo and his nearby estate, where he often was useful as an interpreter in Portuguese.

Do you know: Jacques Cartier stayed with the Indians during winters, two of whom he kidnapped as he returned to France.

15. *Daniel Boone*

Daniel Boone was born on 22nd October 1734 in Pennsylvania and he died on 26th September 1820 (aged 86 years) in Missouri. One of America's first folk heroes Daniel Boone was an expert hunter, marksman and tracker. He made an expedition to the Appalachian Mountains where he started a settlement called Boonesborough and they were regularly attacked by the Shawnee Indians. He eventually moved to Missouri and he enjoyed hunting and the woods till his last days. Daniel Boone remains an iconic figure in American history. He was a legend in his own lifetime.

Do you know: By 1751, Daniel Boone won all the shooting contests he entered. He tracked and killed his first bear at the age of fourteen.

16. *Sacagawea*

Sacagawea was born in May 1788 in the Shoshone tribe, United States, and she died on 20th December 1812 (aged 24 years). As the interpreter and guide for Lewis and Clark Expedition Sacagawea travelled with them through the entire journey to explore Louisiana with her infant tied to her back. Her aide to the expedition was unparalleled as she helped to keep peace and trade with different tribes. At the age of 13, Sacagawea was sold into a non-consensual 'marriage' to Toussaint Charbonneau, a Quebecois trapper living in the village.

Do you know: Impressed with her quick thinking and bravery in rescuing important documents when a boat capsized Lewis and Clark named a river after her.

17. *Henry Hudson*

Henry Hudson was born somewhere in 1565-70, in England, and he died on 22nd June 1611 near Hudson Bay, Canada (North America). The Hudson river and the North Atlantic Oceans were explored and mapped by him when he landed in Maine on his third voyage. This voyage was sponsored by the Dutch. His next voyage was sponsored by the King of England. Both the countries established trading posts and settlements based on his explorations. He spent his entire career searching for different routes to Asia.

Do you know: King James I of England had Henry Hudson put under house arrest for exploring another country after his voyage for the Dutch.

18. *Jacques Cousteau*

Jacques Cousteau was born on 11th June 1910 in France and he died on 25th June 1997 (aged 87 years) in Paris. A French naval officer, explorer, oceanographer, film maker and researcher Jacques Cousteau pioneered Marine Conservation, helped restrict commercial whaling and organized campaigns against the dumping of nuclear waste in the oceans as well as co-invented the 'Aqua Lung', the underwater apparatus that helps divers swim freely for extended periods underwater. He made numerous underwater documentaries, three of which have won the Oscars.

Do you know: Jacques Cousteau started his oceanography career after he had broken both his arms in an accident due to which his career in the French Navy as a pilot was over.

19. Sir Francis Drake

Sir Francis Drake was born in 1540-1544 in Tavistock, England, and he died on 27th January 1596 in Portobelo, Panama. An explorer and a privateer Francis Drake was the first Englishman and second European to sail around the world. On his first voyage to Africa he captured people and sold them as slaves. He became very rich by looting the Spanish ships. He was made the Vice-Admiral of the Navy. At the age of 23, he made his first voyage to the Americas, sailing with his second cousin, Sir John Hawkins, on one of a fleet of ships owned by his relatives.

Do you know: The Spanish called him 'The Dragon' and they put a prize for his capture at 20,000 ducats which is equivalent to seven million dollars today.

20. Samuel de Champlain

Samuel de Champlain was born 13th August 1574 in Brouage, France, and he died on 25th December 1635 (aged 61 years) in Quebec, Canada. An explorer and cartographer who is considered the founder of the Canadian city of Quebec, Samuel helped colonize French North America. Sailing to Canada he became the first European to explore the area, now New York, the site of Montreal, its rapids and further ahead also carrying out fur trade with the local tribes.

Do you know: Samuel de Champlain also explored and wrote about the Niagara Falls which became a popular destination due to his writing.

21. Zheng He

Zheng He was born in 1371 in the Yunnan Province, China, and he died in 1433 (aged 62 years). A great Chinese explorer and fleet commander Zheng He went on seven voyages to establish Chinese trade in new areas. Travelling all the way to Calicut, India, he made trading and diplomatic ties with about 25 countries going as far as Africa and Australia. He also battled pirates on his voyages. His last voyage, to Africa's Swahili coast, with a side trip to Mecca, marked the end of China's golden age of exploration and of Zheng He's life. He presumably died en route home and was buried at sea.

Do you know: Zheng He was captured and taken as a slave to Prince Zhu Di who gave him the name Zheng He. Zheng He was originally called Ma He.

22. *Juan Ponce de Leon*

Juan Ponce de Leon was born in 8 April 1460 in Santervas De Campos, Spain and he died in July 1521 (aged 61 years) in Havana, Cuba. Juan was a Spanish explorer and conquistador. Sailing to the New World Juan became the governor over a section of land which made him rich. In 1506, he reached Puerto Rico and discovered gold and fertile land. Establishing the first Spanish colony he became the first Governor of Puerto Rico. He also discovered a beautiful land and called it 'La Florida'.

Do you know: Juan Ponce joined Christopher Columbus on his second voyage to the New World.

23. *Hernando de Soto*

A Spanish explorer and conquistador Hernando de Soto was born on 27th October 1495 in Spain and he died on 21st May 1542 (aged 47 years) in Ferriday, United States. Credited with discovering the Mississippi River Hernando also explored the parts of the nine states in the United States. In 1514, he assisted in the conquest of Nicaragua and Peru. Hernando de Soto was made the Governor of Cuba. In the May of 1539, he landed in Florida, Georgia and South Carolina moving up to North Carolina and Tennessee. Hernando de Soto died on the banks of the Mississippi River in what is now Guachoya, Arkansas or Ferriday, Louisiana.

Do you know: Hernando's Expedition provided the first documented description of the native people in South-eastern United States.

24. *Reinhold Messner*

Reinhold Messner was born on 17th September 1944 in Brixen, Italy and he still lives there today. An Italian mountaineer, adventurer, explorer and author Reinhold Messner is the first to climb all the 14 independent mountains on the Earth that are more than 8,000 metres high. He has climbed Mount Everest without bottled oxygen, crossed Antarctica on skis and in 2004, completed a 2,000-km expedition through the Gobi desert. He has also done a solo climb to Nanga Parbat. There are 14 peaks on the Earth with summits in the 'dealth zone'. At the age of 42, he became the first person to climb them all.

Do you know: Mountaineer Reinhold Messner has lost the tips of several fingers and seven toes in his life as a climber.

25. *Leif Eriksson*

Leif Eriksson was the son of Erik the Red and born in about 970 in Iceland and he died somewhere in 1020 (50 years) in Greenland. Said to have been the first person ever to have discovered North America when his ship was blown off course Leif Eriksson sighted land on the other side of Greenland and named it Vinland because the land was full of vines and grapes. He made a small settlement there called 'Leif's Booth'. He was commissioned by the King of Norway to spread Christianity.

Do you know: Leif is said to have beaten Christopher Columbus by at least 400 years in discovering America.

26. *Bartolomeu Dias*

Bartolomeu Dias was born in about 1450, Portugal and he died on 29th May 1500 (aged 50 years) at sea near the Cape Town, South Africa. The first European mariner to go round the southernmost tip of Africa around the Cape of Good Hope to enter the Indian Ocean, Bartolomeu opened the sea route to Asia via the Atlantic Ocean which increased the trade with India and other Asian powers. He worked in Guinea, West Africa where Portugal had established a gold trading post. Using his experience with explorative travel, he helped in the construction of the Sao Gabriel and its sister ship, the Sao Rafael.

Do you know: Bartolomeu Dias was employed to be a ship-building consultant for the ships that were used by Vasco da Gama.

27. *Roald Amundsen*

Roald Amundsen was born on 16th July 1872 in Borge, Norway, and he died on 18th June 1928 (aged 56 years), Bear Island, Norway. Roald was a Norwegian explorer of polar regions and he was the leader of the Antarctic expedition of 1910–12. The first man to visit the South Pole, Roald had originally decided to go to the North Pole but Robert Peary reached there before him. So, Roald decided to pursue the South Pole and he finally planted the Norwegian Flag there on 11th December 1911. In 1926, Roald Amundsen and 15 other men made the first crossing of the Arctic in the airship Norge.

Do you know: All five members returned safely but they lost 41 of the 52 dogs in the expedition.

28. *Sir Edmund Hillary*

Sir Edmund Hillary was born on 20th July 1919 in Auckland, New Zealand, and passed away on 11th January 2008 (aged 88-89 years) in Auckland, New Zealand. The first person to climb Mount Everest, along with Tenzing Norgay, they stayed there only a few minutes as the air was so thin. He summited several other Himalayan peaks and was the third person to reach the South Pole over land and the first to do so using motor vehicles. On 6th June 1953 Edmund Hillary was appointed Knight Commander of the Order of the British Empire and received the Queen Elizabeth-II Coronation Medal.

Do you know: Edmund Hillary was knighted by Queen Elizabeth II after reaching Mount Everest; that is why he is referred to as 'Sir'.

29. *Tenzing Norgay*

Tenzing Norgay was born on 29th May 1914 in Khumbu, Solukhumbu District, Sagarmatha Zone, Nepal and he died on 9th May 1986 (aged 72 years) in Darjeeling, West Bengal, India. The first man along with Edmund Hillary to have climbed Mount Everest, Tenzing was a Nepalese mountaineer of Tibetian descent who worked as a porter. He became the organiser of Sherpa guides and was a part of a number of other expeditions that had tried to summit Mount Everest but their expeditions did not succeed. Tenzing participated as a high-altitude porter in three official British attempts to climb Everest from the northern Tibetan side.

Do you know: Tenzing was awarded Britain's George Medal and the Star of Nepal by the Nepalese government for this feat.

30. *Yuri Gagarin*

Yuri Gagarin was born on 9th March 1934 in Klushino, Soviet Union, and he died on 27th March 1968 (aged 34 years) in Kirzhach, Russia. Yuri was the first human to journey into outer space when his spacecraft 'Vostok' completed an orbit of the Earth on 12th April 1961. He was a pilot with the ranking of a colonel in the Soviet Airforce. He joined the Soviet Airforce in 1955 and was training to be an astronaut by 1960. 108-minute flight gave him a permanent place in sie history books as the first man in space. He was a keen sportsman all his life and played ice hockey and was a basketball fan.

Do you know: Yuri Gagarin was awarded the 'Hero of the Soviet', the highest award given in his nation after his successful launch into space.

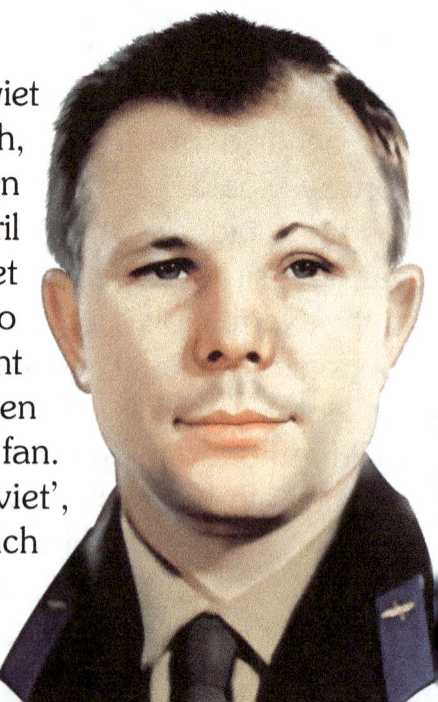

31. *Ibn Battuta*

Abu Abdullah Muhammad Ibn Battuta was born on 25th February 1304 in Tangier, Morocco, and he died in 1369 (aged 65 years) in Morocco. One of the greatest medieval Muslim travellers and authors of one of the most famous travel books entitled 'Rihlah', his work describes his travels covering some 75,000 miles in trips to almost all of the Muslim countries and as far as China and Sumatra. The interiors of the Ibn Battuta Mall in Dubai, UAE, inaugurated in 2005, are inspired by the travels of Ibn Battuta.

Do you know: Ibn Battuta was appointed the Grand Qazi (Judge) of Delhi by Muhammad Bin Tuglak when he came to India.

32. *Gertrude Bell*

Gertrude Bell was born on 14th July 1868 in Washington Hall, England, and she died on 12th July 1926 (aged 58 years) in Baghdad, Iraq. A British traveller, archaeologist and political officer Gertrude explored and mapped her extensive travels through Syria, Mesopotamia, Asia Minor and Arabia. Gertrude was also known as Britain's Queen of the Desert. She played a major role in establishing the modern day Iraq and setting up its National Museum and was fluent in Persian and Arabic. Aged just 20, she was the first woman to achieve a first in history at Lady Margaret Hall, Oxford.

Do you know: Gertrude Bell's writings about her experiences in the Middle East, especially Iraq, are studied and referred to even now by modern day policy-makers.

33. *Ernest Shackleton*

Ernest Shackleton was born on 15th February 1874 in Kilkea, Ireland, and he died on 5th January 1922 (aged 48 years) in South Georgia. A merchant Navy officer, Ernest led three British expeditions to the Antarctic region. During his second expedition his team established a new record by reaching 97 geographical miles from the South Pole which was then the largest advance to the Pole in exploration history. Members of his team also climbed Mount Erebus, the most active Antarctic Volcano. Shackleton Memorial Fund was used for assisting the education of his children and the support of his mother.

Do you know: Knighted by King Edwards VII, Ernest became a hero and was considered a role model.

34. *Sir Walter Raleigh*

Sir Walter Raleigh was born in 1552 in Devon, England, and he died on 29th October 1618 (aged 66 years) in London, England. Sir Walter was an explorer, soldier and writer of much note during the reign of Queen Elizabeth I. He established a colony near Roanoke Island, now North Carolina. He was also famous for his sense of dressing and extremely chivalrous behaviour. He wrote 'History of the World' in 1614 while he was imprisoned in a tower with his wife and servants. Sir Walter was accused of treason by King James I, was imprisoned and eventually put to death.

Do you know: From his voyages Sir Walter Raleigh brought back with him potatoes and tobacco, the two things which were unknown in Europe at the time.

35. *Erik the Red*

Erik Thorvaldsson, known as Erik the Red, was born in 950 in Norway and he died in 1000 (aged 50 years) in Norway. Erik the Red was a settler and explorer and a viking known to have founded the first continuous settlement in Greenland, Erik was exiled from Iceland twice and moved to Greenland. He arrived there and explored the landmass giving names to various places. By 985, his sentence had expired and he returned to Iceland and had convinced several hundred people to settle in Greenland. His colonies survived a deadly epidemic but died out around the time of Columbus.

Do you know: Erik is said to have grown up wild and brazen which coupled with his red hair and beard; it earned him the name Erik the Red.

36. *Peter Minuit*

Peter Minuit was born in 1580 in Wesel, Germany, and he died on 5th August 1638 (aged 58 years) in Saint Christopher, West Indies. Peter Minuit is known for 'purchasing' Manhattan from a native–American tribe in 1626. He was named the director of the New Netherland colony in 1626 which stretches from the present day Delaware into Connecticut. There, he negotiated a deal to buy the Island of Manhattan from the natives. He also developed a flourishing fur trade in the region. Later, he founded a Swedish colony in Delaware Bay by convincing the Swedish Government before his death in a Carribean hurricane.

Do you know: Peter Minuit is said to have purchased Manhattan for 60 guilders which is equivalent of $ 24.

37. *Buzz Aldrin*

Buzz Aldrin or Edwin Eugene Aldrin Jr was born on 20th January 1930 and he is now retired today. An engineer and astronaut, Edwin is known for being the second man to step on the moon following Neil Armstrong. He was an Airforce pilot and was selected by NASA for the Gemini mission in 1969. He later worked on developing space faring technology and became an author writing sci-fi novels, children's books and memoirs including Return to Earth (1973), Magnificent Desolation (2009) and No Dream is Too High: Life Lessons from a Man Who Walked on the Moon (2016).

Do you know: To commemorate the 40th Anniversary of the first lunar landing Edwin teamed up with famous singers like Snoop Dogg, Quincy Jones and others to create a rap single and video called 'Rocket Experience'.

38. *William Anders*

William Alison 'Bill' Anders was born on 17th October 1933 in British Hong Kong and he is now retired from fighter pilot, Major General, USAFR and settled in the US. A former Airforce officer, nuclear engineer and astronaut, William is one of the first people to have orbited the moon. He held various positions in Nuclear Regulatory and Developmental Activities that the US was involved in, including being invited by President Ford to be the first Chairman of the Nuclear Regulatory Commission. Later, he went as the US ambassador to Norway and held that position till 1977.

Do you know: William Anders' picture 'Earthrise' was selected by NASA to represent the mission and later became an iconic shot of the twentieth century.

39. *Harriet Chalmers Adams*

Harriet Chalmers Adams was born on 22th October 1875, Stockton, California, US and she died on 17th July 1937 (aged 62 years) in Nice, France. Harriet was an American explorer, writer and photographer. She made a three-year journey through Central and South America. She travelled 40,000 miles, visiting every country, and reaching many points previously unknown to any white woman. In 1916, Harriet was a war correspondent at the French front, and she returned to the US in 1917 to continue her lectures. In 1925, she organized, and became the first president of the Society of Women Geographers.

Do you know: Harriet wrote regularly for National Geographic and was a fellow and member of various geographical and scientific associations throughout the world.

40. Sir Samuel Baker

Sir Samuel White Baker was born on 8th June 1821 in London, England, and he died on 30th December 1893 (aged 72 years) in Devon, England. Sir Samuel Baker is known to have found the source of the Nile and explored the Nile tributaries around Sudan and the Ethiopian border. He found the source of the Nile to be a lake which he named Lake Albert which is situated between modern Uganda and Congo. He also led an Egyptian Expedition to the Upper Nile to claim the territory for Egypt and to suppress and possibly put an end to the slave trade.

Do you know: Queen Victoria excluded Samuel Baker from the court for marrying Florence Baker as Florence Baker was a slave who had been sold to Samuel Baker.

41. Florence Baker

Florence Baker was born on 6th August 1841 in Hungary and she died on 11th March 1916 (aged 75 years) in Devon, England. Along with Samuel Baker she launched an expedition to find the source of the Nile and found Lake Albert. She saved the expedition by solving the dispute that rose between Samuel Baker and the staff. She later returned to Africa with Samuel Baker, who she married, to try and put down the slave trade.

Do you know: Florence Baker was the daughter of a Hungarian nobleman who was killed during the Hungarian Revolution. She became an orphan who was sold to Samuel Baker as a slave.

42. Thor Heyerdahl

Thor Heyerdahl was born on 6th October 1914 in Larvik, Norway, and he died on 18th April 2002 (aged 87 years) in Italy. Famous for his Kontiki Expedition Thor sailed 8,000-km across the Pacific Ocean in a hand-built raft to prove that the ancient people could make long voyages making contacts with the people of other cultures. He was also an archaeologist who excavated pyramids in Peru and the Canary Islands. In 1955-56, Thor Heyerdahl organized the Norwegian Archaeological Expedition to Rapa Nui (Easter Island).

Do you know: Thor Heyerdahl wrote a book about this famous expedition; the book became an international best-seller and was translated into 65 languages.

43. Kit Carson

Christopher Kit Carson was born on 24th December 1809 in Madison County, Kentucky, and he died on 23rd May 1868 (aged 58 years) in Colorado. An American trapper and guide, Kit Carson made an important contribution to the westward expansion of the United States working on various journeys with many explorers. In 1853, he agreed to work as an Indian agent for northern New Mexico advising on making reservations for the Native Americans to prevent their extinction. He was a mountain man (fur trapper), wilderness guide, Indian guide and US army officer–all in one.

Do you know: Kit Carson grew up on the Missouri frontier which was bought from the sons of Daniel Boone, the famous explorer.

44. Willem Schouten

Willem Cornelisz Schouten was born in 1567, Hoorn, Netherlands and he died in 1625 (aged 58 years), Antongil Bay, Madagascar. He was a dutch explorer and navigator for the Dutch East India Company. In 1615, Willem and his younger brother Jan Schouten sailed from Texel in the Netherlands, in an expedition led by Jacob le Maire and sponsored by Isaac Le Marie. He crossed the Pacific Ocean, discovering a number of coral islands in the Tuamotu Islands. He then followed the north coasts of New Ireland and New Guinea and visited adjacent islands.

Do you know: Willem Cornelisz Schouten was the first explorer to navigate Cape Horn and established a route to get to the Pacific Ocean.

45. Martin Forbisher

Sir Martin Forbisher was born in 1535 in Yorkshire, UK, and he died on 22nd November 1594 (aged 59 years) in Plymouth, UK. Well-known for the discovery of Labrador and Forbisher Bay in Canada, Martin was one of the first English explorers who tried to discover a North-West Passage to the Indies but failed. He was sent back to set up a colony there which he could not do due to dissension and discontent. Martin Forbisher's travels began in the 1505s, when he explored Africa's northwest coast, particularly Guinea.

Do you know: Martin Forbisher became a licensed pirate and used to plunder French ships off the coast of Africa.

46. Gaspar Cortes Real

Gaspar Cortes Real was born in 1450 in the Kingdom of Portugal and he disappeared around 1501. Gaspar was an explorer to the Portuguese King who sent him to discover lands and a North-West Passage to Asia. He reached Greenland instead believing it to be East Asia but chose not to land. He went on another voyage to Greenland with his explorer brother Miguel. Due to frozen seas, they changed course and reached what is now Labrador in Canada where they captured some natives and sold them as slaves.

Do you know: Gaspar Cortes Real sent his brother Miguel back to Portugal and was never heard from again. His brother set out later to find him but he too disappeared.

47. Louis Joliet

Louis Joliet was born on 21st September 1645 in Quebec, Canada, and he died in May 1700 (aged 55 years) in Canada. Louis was a Canadian explorer who explored the origin of the Mississippi river with the help of Native American tribes, he embarked on this expedition with Jacques Marquette and became one of the first Europeans to explore the Mississippi river. On the way back, Louis took a short cut along the rapids of Lachine where he was almost drowned.

Do you know: Louis became famous by late 17th century for his expeditions from which official regional maps were created. He had become a professor of hydrography in the University of Quebec for some years before he died.

48. Robert Peary

Robert Edwin Peary was born on 6th May 1856 in Pennsylvania and he died on 20th February 1920 (aged 64 years) in Washington DC. Robert reached the Geographic North Pole with his expedition on 6th April 1909. Robert Peary made his first expedition to the Arctic hoping to cross by a dog-sled. He and a companion travelled nearly a 100 miles before turning back due to lack of food. He made it finally in the expedition in 1909.

Do you know: Robert Edwin Peary's claim was debated as the same was claimed by Frederick Cook who said that he got there a year earlier. It is suspected that he may have been 30-60 miles short of the Pole, but he's still given credit for the same.

49. *Mungo Park*

Mungo Park was born on 11th September 1771 in Selkirk, Scotland and he died in January 1806 (aged 35 years) in Bussa, Nigeria. The first westerner to travel to find the source of the Niger River, Mungo wrote about this expedition which became very popular. On the journey he was held prisoner by a Moorish chief for four months, escaping with only a horse and traced the river following it for 300 miles. His book encouraged many to follow him on this path as he had introduced a vast unknown continent.

Do you know: Mungo Park was a trained surgeon who worked aboard an East India Company's ship and as a physician when he settled in Peebles.

50. *John Galt*

John Galt was born on 2nd May 1779 in Irvine, Scotland, and he died on 11th April 1839 (aged 60 years) in Greenock, Scotland. Appointed to aid the colonization of Canada, John opened roads through the thick forests between Lakes Huron and Erie and founded the cities of Guelph and Goderich. He explored and travelled to the Mediterranean and Europe extensively. He was later dismissed and recalled to England where he was imprisoned for several months. John Galt was the father of Sir Alexander Tilloch Galt of Montreal, Quebec.

Do you know: John Galt was a very successful writer who wrote about the rural life of Scotland. His famous novels are: 'Sir Andrew Wylie', 'Annals of the Parish' and 'Ringan Gilhaize'.

51. *Richard Evelyn Byrd*

Richard Evelyn Byrd was born on 25th October 1888 in Winchester, Virginia, and he died on 11th March 1957 (aged 68 years) in Boston, Massachusetts. The first person to reach the South Pole by air, Richard completed the distance in 18 hours and 41 minutes. He was an American naval officer and polar explorer. He has been a leader and navigator in expeditions, and has crossed the Atlantic Ocean and a segment of both the Arctic Ocean and the Antarctic Plateau. His claim to have reached the North Pole is disputed.

Do you know: Richard Evelyn Byrd has been awarded the 'Medal of Honour' and was the youngest admiral in the history of US Navy.

52. *Joseph Banks*

Joseph Banks was born on 24th February 1743 in London, UK, and he died on 19th June 1820 (aged 77 years) in London, UK. Joseph was a Botanist, scientist and explorer. He explored the newly discovered areas of New Foundland and Labrador and even went as far as Iceland to study the natural history of these places. He published the first account of the flora and fauna of this area. A part of the first voyage was undertaken by James Cook where on landing in Brazil he made the first scientific description of the commom garden plant, Bougainvillea.

Do you know: More than 80 species of plants and a group of Islands are named after Joseph Banks.

53. *Pedro de Alvarado*

Pedro de Alvarado was born in about 1485 in Badojoz, Spain, and he died on 4th July 1541 (aged 56 years) in Guadalajara, Mexico. A Spanish conquistador and Second-in-command to Hernan Cortes in the expedition for the conquest of Mexico, Pedro occupied the Aztec capital. He was also sent to take over the Mayans and other smaller kingdoms by either making them surrender or fight. He became the governor of this area which is now Guatemala.

Do you know: Pedro de Alvarado was a handsome man with a blond beard and hair which earned him the nickname 'Tonatiuh' from the Aztecs which meant the Sun but he was also known to be extremely cruel to the local population.

54. *Richard Francis Burton*

Sir Richard Francis Burton was born on 19th March 1821 in Torquay, Devon, England, and he died on 20th October 1890 (aged 69 years) in Trieste, Hungary. The first European to visit the Great Lakes of Africa, Richard and his companion were the first to reach Lake Tanganyika. He wrote a well-documented trip to the Mecca, translated the Arabian Nights into English and took to learning about the Indian culture and learnt all the intricacies of it.

Do you know: Sir Richard Francis Burton could speak many languages including French, Italian, Neapolitan, Latin and Arabic. His repertoire also included Sindhi, Punjabi, Gujarati, Marathi and Persian.

55. Rene Robert Cavelier

Rene Robert Cavelier, Sieur de La Salle, or Robert de La Salle was born on 22nd November 1643 in Rouen, Normandy, France, and he died on 19th March 1687 (aged 43 years) in Huntsville, Texas. Rene is known for leading an expedition to the Mississippi river and claiming the area for France. He named it Louisiana after King Louis XIV. Along the way in this expedition he built Fort Prod'homme at the present day Memphis. On his return trip he established another fort in Illinois called Fort Louis. His expeditions built a network of forts from Canada across the Great Lakes moving into Ohio, Illinois and the Mississippi rivers. This gave the French a stronghold in the New World.

Do you know: Rene gave up his inheritance at the age of 15 to become a Jesuit priest.

56. Vasco Nunez de Balboa

Vasco Nunez de Balboa was born in 1475 in Spain and he died on 12th January 1519 (aged 44 years) in Acla, Panama. A Spanish Explorer and conquistador Vasco was the first European to have crossed the Isthmus of Panama to see the Pacific Ocean. He also established the town of Darien on the Isthmus of Panama where he also became the interim governor of the settlement. He also explored and conquered the Mar del Sur and its surrounding lands.

Do you know: While Vasco Nunez de Balboa was exploring the high seas the King of Spain sent Pedro Arias de Avila as the new Governor of Darien. Pedro being jealous of Vasco had him arrested and beheaded for treason.

57. Gonzalo Pizarro

Gonzalo Pizarro was born in 1510 in Trujillo, Spain, and he died on 10th April 1548 (aged 38 years) in Cuzco, Peru. Gonzalo travelled with his half brother Francisco Pizarro on his expedition to Peru and helped him take over the Incas and overthrow the Incan ruler for which he was rewarded by Spain with land and he was made governor of Quito. Later, he led a rebellion against the Spanish Government which made new rules to curb the abuse by Spanish Colonists and improve the life of the natives. Gonzalo Pizarro headed this rebellion and he had to surrender after his troops had abandoned him. He was beheaded for this.

Do you know: Gonzalo is considered the first leader of the struggle by colonists for independence from Spanish domination in America.

58. Bartolome de Las Casas

Bartolome de Las Casas was born in 1484 in Sevilla, Spain, and he died on 18th July 1566 (aged 82 years) in Madrid, Spain. A Spanish missionary, Bartolome travelled to the western hemisphere to take care of the lands that were given to his father by Christopher Columbus, moving to West Indies and working towards the betterment of the natives. He is one of the earliest people who worked for human rights. He became the first resident Bishop of Chiapas, and the first officially appointed 'Protector of the Indians'.

Do you know: Bartolome de Las Casas wrote a massive book 'History of the Indies' which he finished in 1562 but it was published only in 1875. It included an invaluable extract of Columbus' first logbook.

59. Juan de Onate

Juan de Onate was born in 1550 in Zacatecas City, Mexico and he died on 3rd June 1626 (aged 76 years) in Seville, Spain. Juan de Onate established the colony of New Mexico for Spain. His request to conquer and govern New Mexico was approved in 1595 but his expedition started only three years later. This became one of Spain's most important outposts and he was named the governor. Juan de Onate was considered a failure by his monarch because the colony did not prosper and the natives revolted. He spent a lot of time looking for the riches in North America which did not exist and ended up exploring what is now the south western United States.

Do you know: Juan de Onate was married to the grand-daughter of Hernan Cortes, the famous explorer and the great-grand daughter of the Aztec King.

60. Diego Velazquez de Cuellar

Diego Velazquez de Cuellar was born in 1465 in Cuellar, Spain, and he died in 12th June 1524 (aged 59 years) in Cuba. Diego was involved in the second voyage of Christopher Columbus to America. He also sailed to Cuba to conquer it with Hernan Cortes in 1511 and founded four settlements there including Santiago de Cuba and Havana. He encouraged colonization and became the Governor of Cuba. He became interested in the exploration of Mexico for which he sent ships and men under the order of Cortes who founded the Veracruz on the Mexican Gulf after which he repudiated his authority.

Do you know: Diego Velazquez de Cuellar complained about Cortes but was asked to ignore Cortes; it broke his heart and he pined away.

61. Abel Janszoon Tasman

Abel Janszoon Tasman was born in 1603 in Lutjegast, Netherlands and he died on 10th October 1659 (aged 56 years) in Batavia, Dutch East Indies. Abel is best known for his voyages of 1642 and 1644 during which he discovered the islands of Van Diemen's Land (now Tasmania) and New Zealand. On his second voyage, in 1644, he followed the south coast of New Guinea eastward. He missed Strait Torres between New Guinea and Australia, and continued his voyage along the Australian coast. He mapped the north coast of Australia.

Do you know: At the northern end of the South Island, Abel Janszoon Tasman anchored the ships in a bay, where in his only encounter with the Maori four of his sailors were killed.

62. Friar Andres de Urdaneta

Friar Andres de Urdaneta was born on 30th November 1498 in Villafranca de Oria, Spain, and he died on 3rd June 1568 (aged 70 years), in Mexico City. Friar Andres spent eight adventurous years in the Spice Islands (Moluccas) and then, in 1553, entered the Augustinian order in Mexico City. Philip II of Spain asked him to guide an expedition from Mexico to the Philippines and to find a return route. In April 1565, Friar Andres reached the Philippine island of Cebu, where he established a mission, and on 1st June 1565 he embarked on the return voyage.

Do you know: Friar Andres de Urdaneta was one of the few survivors of the Loaísa Expedition to reach the Spice Islands late in the year 1526, only to be taken prisoner by the Portuguese.

63. Diego de Almagro

Diego de Almagro was born in 1475 in Almagro, Spain, and he died on 8th July 1538 (aged 63 years) in Cusco, Peru. Diego was the first European to discover Chile when he participated in the Spanish conquest of Peru. He led the expedition that conquered the Inca empire along with Francisco Pizarro but there was much instability in the new colony because of friction between the two captains. Later, Diego de Almagro was chosen by the King of Spain to assist in the conquest of Chile where he suffered many hardships.

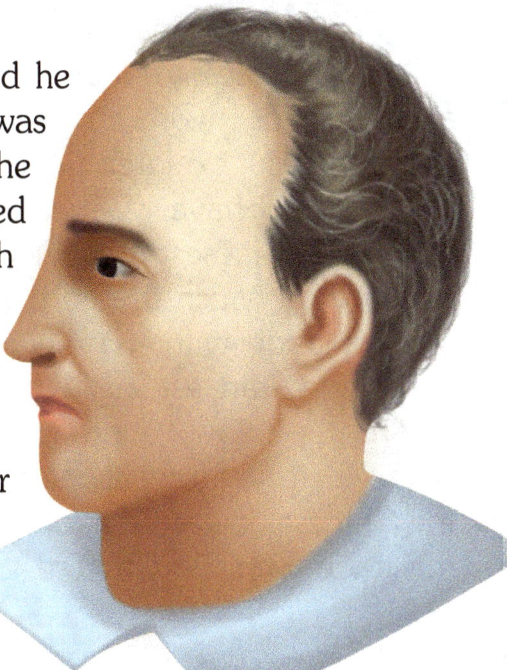

Do you know: A dear friend of Francisco Pizarro they later turned into the most bitter rivals. After defeating Diego's army for imprisoning his brothers Francisco put him to death.

64. *Francisco de Almeida*

Francisco de Almeida was born in 1450 in Lisbon, Portugal, and he died on 1st March 1510 (aged 60 years) in the Cape of Good Hope. Francisco was a Portuguese Explorer and soldier who was responsible for the Portuguese dominance over the Indian Ocean. The King of Portugal appointed Francisco the first governor and Viceroy of the Portuguese State of India. He was to bring the spice trade of India under their control and to construct forts along the Indian coasts. He did the same in Africa and captured Zanzibar for Portugal. He became a soldier at a young age, fought in Morocco and was a part of the Christian conquest of Granada.

Do you know: Francisco defeated the Ottomans and the Egyptians to avenge the death of his son and reinstated the Portuguese monopoly.

65. *Benedict Allen*

Benedict Collin Allen was born on 1st March 1960 in Cheshire, England, and he still lives there. Benedict is an author, adventurer, film maker and explorer. He is best known for his techniques of mingling with the indigenous people from whom he learns survival skills. His expeditions include a trip to a volcano in Costa Rica, a remote forest in Brunei, a glacier in Iceland and the most epic being an independent journey through the least known regions of the Amazon and New Guinea and many more such adventures.

Do you know: Benedict Collin Allen has pioneered the use of a headheld camera for TV. He has been for many years the first and only television adventurer.

66. *Jorge Alvares*

Jorge Alvares was born in the late 15th century in Portugal and he died on 8th July 1521 in Tamao, China. Jorge was a Portuguese explorer who is credited with being the first European to have reached China by sea. He made contact with the Chinese when they landed on the historic city of Guangzhou which the Portuguese called Tamao. They hoped to start trade with the Chinese. Jorge later also joined the venture to start establishing settlements in Tamao.

Do you know: Although Jorge Alvares and following him Rafael Perestrello were the first people to make contact with the Chinese, it was Fernao Pires de Andrade who really started the trade with the Chinese.

67. *Antonio de Andrade*

Antonio de Andrade was born in 1580 in Oleiros, Portugal, and he died on 19th March 1634 (aged 54 years) in Goa Velha. Antonio was an explorer and a Jesuit priest. He was the first person to cross the Himalayas to reach Tibet where he was the first to establish a Catholic mission. Antonio and a fellow Jesuit priest joined the group of Hindu pilgrims and reached the Badrinath temple in the Northern part of India and from there they crossed the Mana pass into Tibet. He also wrote two accounts of his experiences in Tibet in Portuguese; his accounts were translated into all major European languages.

Do you know: Antonio was attached to the court of the Mughal Emperor Jahangir and was the head of the Jesuit mission in Agra and Goa.

68. *Henryk Arctowski*

Henryk Arctowski was born on 21st July 1871 in Warsaw, Poland, and he died on 21st February 1958 (aged 87 years) in Bethesda, United States. A Polish scientist and explorer who was the first person to spend winters in the Antarctic region where Henryk performed scientific work and observations himself with just an assistant. Various geographical features have been named after him. He published more than 144 papers in geophysics and geodesy. He was also instrumental in restoring Polish Independence after World War I.

Do you know: Henryk Arctowski could never return to Poland and lost all his possessions after the Nazi had attacked Poland.

69. *Salomon August Andree*

Salomon August Andree was born on 18th October 1854 in Granna, Sweden, and he died in October 1897 (aged 43 years) in Kvitoya. Salomon was a Swedish engineer, physicist, aeronaut and explorer. He is best known for attempting to reach the North Pole by a hydrogen balloon. This expedition was unsuccessful and led to the deaths of all three participants. He was also a participant in the Swedish expedition where he was responsible for observations regarding air electricity. He published scientific journals about air electricity, conduction of heat and inventions.

Do you know: The remains of the three men were finally found in 1930 by the Norwegian expedition. Their notebooks, diaries and photographic negatives and other objects were also found.

70. *Roy Chapman Andrews*

Roy Chapman Andrews was born on 26th January 1884 in Beloit, Wisconsin, United States and he died on 11th March 1960 (aged 76 years) in Carmel-by-the-Sea, California, United States. A renowned naturalist, Roy led expeditions into the Gobi desert and Mongolia. He brought back the first known dinosaur's eggs and numerous precious fossils. Roy travelled to the Arctic where he filmed some of the best footage of seals ever seen. He has written various books about his expeditions, and his own life.

Do you know: Roy Chapman Andrews wanted to work in the Museum of Natural history so badly that on being told that there was no opening he took a job as a janitor in the Museum.

71. *Vladimir Arsenyev*

Vladimir Klavdiyevich Arsenyev was born on 10th September 1872 in Saint Petersburg, Russia, and he died on 4th September 1930 (aged 58 years) in Vladivostok, Russia. Vladimir is known for documenting and describing the various species of Siberian flora and the lifestyle of the ethnic people. He undertook many expeditions where he acutely studied the natural flora of the region. He authored many books on geography, wildlife and ethnography of the regions. His most famous book entitled 'Ussurian Taiga' was named after Arsenyev's guide, a native of Nanai tribe. The book was eventually made into two films, one of which even won the Oscar Award for the best foreign language film.

Do you know: Vladimir's wife was arrested soon after his death and executed for being a spy. His daughter was sent to a labour camp.

72. *Vaino Auer*

Vaino Auer was born on 7th January 1895 in Helsinki, Finland, and he died on 20th March 1981 (aged 86 years) in Helsinki, Finland. Auer was a professor of geography at the University of Helsinki. Vaino expert in swamp geology, he documented the Earth's climatic history and explored the areas of Tierra del Fuego and Patagonia. He also advised the Argentinian government in the matters of land use and the colonization of the Southern part of the Argentina. In the last year of his professional career he served as a professor of geography (1953-57), and of geology and palaeontology.

Do you know: Through the notes in Vaino Auer, diary and articles written by him he is said to have been involved in the construction of a German submarine base in Tierra del Fuego.

73. *George Back*

Admiral Sir George Back was born on 6th November 1796 in Cheshire, UK, and he died on 23rd June, 1878 (aged 81 years) in London, UK. A British Naval Admiral, naturalist and artist, George was an explorer who is remembered to have explored the Canadian Arctic. His expedition to the Canadian Arctic was a proposition to find explorer John Ross who had gone missing in that area. George volunteered to take the fur trade route to the Great Fish River where no European had gone before. This river was later named Back River after Sir George Back.

Do you know: Sir George Back was a skilled artist and his work sold at high prices.

74. *William Baffin*

William Baffin was born in 1584 in London, United Kingdom and he died on 23rd January 1622 (aged 38 years) in Qesham, Iran. William was a navigator, best known for his attempt to discover a passage in the Northwest from the Atlantic to the Pacific Ocean. He is also well known for the accuracy of his many scientific and magnetic observations. His calculation of Longitude at sea by Lunar observation is the first of its kind on record. William sailed various expeditions with a number of captains to explore areas such as Greenland where he discovered a bay which has been named after him. His journals are the only account of several of his voyages.

Do you know: William Baffin had a few Islands in Greenland and a variety of the rose named after him.

75. *Robert Ballard*

Robert Duane Ballard was born on 30th June 1942 in Kansas, USA and he still lives there today. He is most well-known for his discovery of the Titanic. Robert is noted for his work in Marine archaeology. He also discovered the Battleship Bismarck, the aircraft carrier USS Yorktown and the wreck of John Fitzgerald Kennedy's plane. His first expedition to find the Titanic in 1977 was unsuccessful. In his next attempt, he sought the help of the US Navy which requested him to look for their two sunken submarines first. He finally found the wreck of Titanic on the morning of 1st September 1985.

Do you know: Robert Duane Ballard attributed his interest in underwater exploration after reading the classic novel '20,000 Leagues under the Sea'.

76. *Giosafat Barbaro*

Giosafat Barbaro was born in 1413 in Venice, Italy, and he died in 1494 (aged 81 years) in Venice, Italy. Giosafat was a diplomat, travel writer and explorer. He was a member of the influential Barbaro family of Venice. He travelled extensively for the times he lived in. Giosafat's account of his travels provides more information than any other account from his times. He had travelled to Tana, a Genoese colony, many cities in Crimea, Cyprus, Germany, Poland and Russia before he returned to Venice. His writings included political matters, commerce, agriculture and customs of the places he visited.

Do you know: Giosafat Barbaro was a diplomat, merchant, explorer and travel writer. His writings were first published in 1543 and they have been translated into English, Russian and Turkish.

77. *Nicolas Baudin*

Nicolas Thomas Baudin was born on 17th February 1754 in France and he died on 16th September 1803 (aged 49 years) in Mauritius. Nicolas was a French explorer, cartographer and naturalist. He undertook the expedition to map the coast of New Holland, now Australia. The aim of the expedition was to research and observe the geography and the natural history of the place. They reached Tasmania and interacted with the locals and made the studies of these people. He made a survey of the east coast and named a lot of places that he discovered.

Do you know: Nicolas Baudin is known to have prepared a report for Napolean Bonaparte on ways to invade the British Colony at Sydney Cove.

78. *William Beebe*

William Beebe was born on 29th July 1877 in New York, USA, and he died on 4th June 1962 (aged 85 years) in Trinidad. William was a naturalist who was known for his deep dives in Bathyspheres to study marine animals and his study of the world's pheasants. He founded a research station in Trinidad where research still continues. He is considered the founder of 'ecology' and conservation. He had also proposed the theory of 'Avian Evolution'. William Beebe wrote over 800 articles and 24 books on natural history.

Do you know: In his career, William has 64 animals named after him and has described one new species of birds and 87 species of fish.

79. *Pyotr Beketov*

Pyotr Beketov was born in 1600, in Russia and he died in 1661 (aged 61 years) in Tobolsk, Russia. The founder of many cities, Pyotr was sent to Siberia and was the first Russian to enter Buryatia where he founded the first Russian settlement. He was in military service and was sent to Siberia from where he proceeded on his first voyage to Zabaykalye to collect taxes. They further founded Yakutsk to be used as a base for further expeditions eastwards. After his second voyage to Buryatia, he founded Chita, a winter settlement and in the following year the Nerchinsk. He established several more forts and collected taxes. In 1640 he transported the duties he had collected and was appointed a Cossack commander.

Do you know: In 1655, Pyotr was attacked by the Buryats and they barely managed to escape with their lives.

80. *Fabian Gottlieb von Bellingshausen*

Fabian Gottlieb von Bellingshausen was born on 20th September 1778 in Estonia and he died on 25th January 1852 (aged 74 years) in Kronstadt, Russia. A Russian naval officer, who discovered the continent of Antarctica, Fabian also participated in the first Russian circumnavigation of the globe. After the expedition, he published a collection of maps of the newly explored area in the Pacific Ocean. Fabian Gottlieb von Bellingshausen is remembered as one of the greatest admirals and explorers in the Russian history. As a prominent cartographer, Fabian Gottlieb was appointed to command the Russian circumnavigation of the globe in 1819-21.

Do you know: In Antarctica multiple geographical features and locations are named after Fabian Gottlieb von Bellingshausen.

81. *Ranulph Fiennes*

Sir Ranulph Twisleton Wykeham Fiennes was born on 7th March 1944 in Windsor, England, and he still lives there today. Ranulph was a British officer, adventurer and explorer. He was the first person to visit both the South and North Poles by surface means. He was also the first person to cross Antarctica on foot. Ranulph undertook numerous other expeditions including climbing Mount Everest at the age of 64. He went on an expedition to the white Nile in a hovercraft. He holds several endurance records. According to the Guinness Book of World Records in 1984, he was the world's greatest living explorer.

Do you know: Sir Ranulph Fiennes ran seven marathons in seven days on seven continents, four months after a double bypass surgery.

82. Joseph Rene Bellot

Joseph Rene Bellot was born on 18th March 1826 in Paris, France, and he died on 18th August 1853 (aged 27 years) in Wellington Channel, Canada. An Arctic explorer, Joseph went on the second expedition to the Arctic to search for Sir John Franklin. During his two years' tour of duty he was wounded and nominated for Legion of honour. He developed an interest in his search of Sir John Franklin and went on the second expedition to the Arctic to look for him. Joseph teamed up with William Kennedy in his sledging operation which promoted the Anglo-French friendship. He was very popular with his shipmates for his kindness and vivacity and devotion to duty.

Do you know: Joseph Rene Bellot was so popular that after his death people contributed to help his impoverished family and made a memorial for him.

83. Benjamin of Tudela

Benjamin of Tudela was born in 1130 in Tudela, Spain, and he died in 1173 (aged 53 years) in Castile, Spain. Benjamin was a Jewish traveller who visited Europe, Asia and Africa in the 12th century. He is an important person in the history of the medieval times because of his knowledge of languages. He wrote extensively about his travels in a book entitled 'The Travels of Benjamin'. He gave the accurate descriptions of the everyday life of the people of those times. He gave detailed descriptions about each city and country he visited and all the landmarks that he saw.

Do you know: Benjamin of Tudela work was originally written in Hebrew but has been translated first into Latin and later into major European languages.

84. Maurice Benyovszky

Maurice Benyovszky was born on 20th September 1746 in Vrbove, Slovakia and he died on 24th May 1786 (aged 40 years) in Ambohitralanana, Madagascar. A Hungarian nobleman, writer and military officer, Moric was offered the privilege to colonize Madagascar where he proclaimed himself King of Madagascar. Later, he came to America where he proposed the use of Madagascar as a base against the British in the American War of Independence. He died fighting the French on Madagascar.

Do you know: Maurice Benyovszky was a military officer in the French, Polish, Austrian and American armies and is considered a national hero in Hungary, Slovakia and Poland.

85. *Vitus Bering*

Vitus Jonassen Bering was born on 5th August 1681 in Denmark and he died on 19th December 1741 (aged 60 years) in Bering Island, Russia. Vitus was the leader of two Russian expeditions exploring the North-eastern coast of Asia and the Western coast of North America to map new areas. He undertook the second trip and sailed to North America. They discovered the Kodiak Island. The record of the wildlife and several plant species they encountered were recorded in detail. Vitus died on this expedition possibly due to scurvy.

Do you know: Bering Strait, Bering Sea, Bering Island, Bering Glacier and the Bering Land Bridge were all named after him in his honour.

86. *Hiram Bingham III*

Hiram Bingham III was born on 19th November 1875 in Honolulu, Hawaii, and he died on 6th June 1956 (aged 81 years) in Washington DC, USA. An explorer, academic and politician, Hiram made the existence of the Inca citadel in Macchu Pichhu known to the public in 1911. He was also one of the pioneers of teaching and research on Latin American history in the US. He published an account of his trip across South America entitled 'Lost city of the Incas' which was a best-seller. He organized the Yale Peruvian Expedition with the aim to find the last Inca capital. Macchu Picchu is a major world attraction and Hiram is considered the man to have brought it fame.

Do you know: Hiram was served as the Governor of Connecticut for the shortest term of one day before being reelected for a full six-year term.

87. *John Blashford-Snell*

Colonel John Blashford-Snell was born on 22nd October 1936 in Hereford, UK, and he is now aged 81 years. John is a former British Army officer, explorer and author. He went to Sandhurst, then joined the Royal Engineers, returning to Sandhurst as adventure training officer, to run expeditions in the Army. He founded the Operation Raleigh and the Scientific Exploration Society. He is credited with inventing White water Rafting, by accident while descending the Blue Nile in 1968. John published many books which include an autobiography. He has been awarded various awards and medals over the years.

Do you know: John Blashford-Snell helped the London hatmakers James & Co to design a hat which would be suitable for the needs of explorers.

88. Adriaen Block

Adriaen Block was born in 1567 in Amsterdam, Netherlands, and he died in 1627 (aged 60 years) in Amsterdam, Netherlands. Adriaen was best known for exploring the coastal and river valley areas between New Jersey and Massachusetts of the present day. He also set up colonies in Connecticut which were the first ones for that area. Adriaen sailed on the Connecticut river and created the Dutch base that later became Hartford. After his return, he made the map for his voyages in 1614; it shows a lot of features which had not appeared in any map of this region before.

Do you know: Adriaen Block is said to have named Rhode Island, Block Island and Fischers Island, after his friend.

89. Vittorio Bottego

Vittorio Bottego was born on 29th July 1860 in Parma, Italy, and he died on 17th March 1897 (aged 37 years) in Ethiopia. Vittorio was an Italian army officer and one of the first Europeans to explore Jubaland which is now in Somalia. He led two expeditions there. In the first expedition, he traced the tributaries of the Ganale Doria River. During his second expedition, he explored the unknown region of upper Juba. He was the first European to follow River Omo to its confluence with Lake Turkana.

Do you know: Vittorio Bottego was killed by the Oromo tribe and the account of his expedition was given by two of his companions, Vannutelli and Citerni, who were kept prisoners for two years by the Emperor of Ethiopia but survived.

90. Saint Brendan

Saint Brendan was born in 484 AD in Feint, Ireland, and he died in 577 AD (aged 93 years) in Annaghdown, Ireland. Saint Brendan was also known as 'The Navigator', 'The Voyager', 'The Anchorite' and 'The Bold'. Little reliable information is found on Saint Brendan but mention of him as a seafarer is given in certain books and Irish genealogies. He founded a number of monasteries, first of which he found in Arran where his first voyage took him. He also visited Columbia, Wales and Britanny on the North coast of France. He set out on his most famous seven-year voyage looking for Paradise.

Do you know: Saint Brendan is one of the 'Twelve Apostles of Ireland'. He is primarily renowned for his legendary quest to the 'Isle of the Blessed', also denominated 'Saint Brendan's Island'.

91. *James Felix Bridger*

James Felix Bridger was born on 17th March 1804 at Virginia, USA, and he died on 17th July 1881 (aged 77 years) in Missouri, USA. James was an explorer, trapper and guide who explored the Western United States. He is credited with discovering the Great Salt Lake in Utah. He mediated between the Native tribes and the Whites who came there either to explore or trade. He came to know many of the major explorers of the region like Kit Carson, Giles Robert, Hugh Glass etc. He even followed the route pioneered by the Lewis-Clark Expedition in 1804.

Do you know: After trapping for leading fur companies, James realised by 1840 that the supply of fur was nearly exhausted.

92. *James Bruce*

James Bruce was born on 14th December 1730 in Stirlingshire, United Kingdom and died on 27th April 1794 (aged 63 years) in Scotland, United Kingdom. James was a Scottish traveller and travel writer who traced the origins of the Blue Nile. He was first commissioned to study the ancient ruins of Algiers. Afterwards, he travelled to Tunis, Tripoli and reached Crete and moved on to Syria. He made the careful drawings of all his ruins which were a part of the Royal collection at Windsor Castle. His next aim was to discover the source of the Blue Nile which he reached on 4th November 1770.

Do you know: James negated Jesuit Pedro Paez's claim to have found the origin of the Blue Nile by saying that the missionary's memoirs had been fabricated.

93. *William Speirs Bruce*

William Speirs Bruce was born 1st August 1867 in London, England, and he died on 28th October 1921 (aged 54 years) in Edinburgh, United Kingdom. William was a Scottish naturalist, polar scientist and oceanographer who led the first and only Scottish National Antarctic Expedition. He set up the first weather station in Antarctica which was recognized as being the foundation for the studies of modern climatic changes. Between 1907 and 1920 he made many journeys to the Arctic regions, both for scientific and for commercial purposes. He founded the Scottish Oceanographical Laboratory in Edinburgh.

Do you know: William was awarded many honours but the Polar Medal due to his enmity with Sir Clements Markham, the president of the Royal Geographical Society on whose recommendation the Medal was given.

94. *Etienne Brule*

Etienne Brule was born in 1592 in Champigny-sur-Marne, France, and he died in June 1633 (aged 41 years), Great Lakes, Canada. Etienne was the first European explorer to journey beyond the Saint Lawrence river into what is today Canada. He explored the Georgian bay and Huron Lake and Humber river which is in today's Toronto. He lived with the Indians to learn their language and their ways. He worked as a guide and interpreter with Samuel de Champlain who also sent Brule on a number of exploratory missions.

Do you know: Etienne Brule has left no description of his explorations and his work has only been recognized through the mention in the works of Champlain, Sagard and Brebeuf.

95. *Frederick Russel Burnham*

Frederick Russel Burnham was born on 11th May 1861 in Minnesota, United States, and he died on 1st September 1947 (aged 86 years) in Santa Barbara, California, United States. Frederick was an American scout and explorer who travelled the world. He is known for his services in colonial Africa for the British Army and the British South Africa Company. Frederick was given the highest military honours earned by any American in the Boer War. After returning to the US, he got involved in National Defence efforts, business, oil, conservation and the Boy Scouts of America.

Do you know: Despite being an American Frederick's military title was British.

96. *Johann Ludwig Burckhardt*

Johann Ludwig Burckhardt was born on 24th November 1784 (aged 33 years) in Lausanne, Switzerland, and he died on 15th October 1817 in Cairo, Egypt. Johann was a Swiss traveller and orientalist who is best known for rediscovering the ruins of the ancient Nabataean city of Petra in Jordan. He studied the Arabic customs and language to the extent that he took on an identity of Sheikh Ibrahim Ibn Abdullah. He wrote extensive details about his journeys and sent his journals back to England from time to time, so all of the details of his travels are secure. He left his large collection of Arabic manuscripts to Cambridge University.

Do you know: Johann was buried as a Muslim and the tombstone over his grave bears the name he assumed on his travels to Arabia–Sheikh Ibrahim Ibn Abd Allah.

97. *Jose de Bustamante y Guerra*

Jose de Bustamante y Guerra was born on 1st April 1759 in Corvera de Toranzo, Spain and he died on 10th March 1825 (aged 66 years) in Madrid, Spain. Jose was a Spanish naval officer, explorer and politician. He along with Alessandro Malaspina proposed a scientific expedition after the voyages of James Cook. They sailed through all the Spanish Colonies and explored the little known areas such as New Zealand and Australia. They explored and mapped the present day Chile and Peru. They kept a diary and their work was published in 1868. Jose was promoted to naval Brigadier and appointed Governor of Paraguay and Montevideo.

Do you know: Jose was captured by the British Squardon while sailing to Spain but was eventually released.

98. *Alvar Nunez Cabeza de Vaca*

Alvar Nunez Cabeza de Vaca was born around 1490 in Jerez de la Frontera, Spain and he died 27 May 1559 (aged 69 years), Sevilla, Spain. Alvar is very well-known as the exploration of the New World and one of the four survivors of the 1527 Narvaez Expedition. He spent 8 years in the gulf region of today's Texas, Arizona and New Mexico. He worked towards the better treatment of the natives and pushed for reforms and advocated policy changes. He authored the first European narrative about North America, providing an anthropological look into the culture of the native Americans.

Do you know: Alvar Nunez Cabeza's book is considered a major contribution to Chicano or Mexican-American Literature. His account is the first written description of the American South-West.

99. *Pedro Alvares Cabral*

Pedro Alvarez Cabral was born in 1467 in Belmonte, Portugal, and he died in 1520 (aged 53 years) in Santarem, Portugal. Pedro is considered the discoverer of Brazil. He was a military commander and explorer who conducted the first significant exploration of the North-east coast of South America and claimed it for Portugal. He was the first sailor to touch all four continents: Europe, Africa, America and Asia. He landed in South America in the area, now known as Brazil. After the discovery of Brazil the ships moved on towards Africa and then hit India by the route that was discovered by Vasco da Gama.

Do you know: When Pedro reached Calicut and started trade, the Arabs attacked them and killed about 50 of his men to maintain their trade monopoly.

100. Juan Rodriguez Cabrillo

Juan Rodriguez Cabrillo was born on 13th March 1499 in Portugal and he died on 3rd January 1543 (aged 44 years) in California, USA. Juan was an explorer and navigator who is known for exploring the West Coast of America for the Spanish empire. He was the first European to navigate the present day California in the United States. He was a part of the conquest of Cuba and later was a part of the battle against the Aztecs in Mexico. He became very rich by mining gold and trading goods as well as slave trade.

Do you know: Juan was sent to arrest Hernan Cortes but he joined Herman Cortes when he couldn't arrest him in his assault of the Aztec Capital.

101. Prince Henry, the Navigator

Prince Henry the Navigator was born on 4th March 1394, Porto, Portugal and he died on 13th November 1460 (aged 66 years) in Sagres, Portugal. Prince Henry, the navigator was a Portuguese explorer and soldier. He sent many expeditions from Portugal to the west coast of Africa, and was responsible for Portugal's influence in the Great Age of Exploration. His expeditions were sent to create much-needed maps of the West African coast, to defeat the Muslims, to spread Christianity, and to establish trade routes. He helped begin the Great Age of Discovery that lasted from the 1400's to the early 1500's. Henry is regarded as the patron of Portuguese exploration.

Do you know: Prince Henry, the Navigator was the third son of King John I and he was responsible for the early development of Portuguese exploration.

102. Rene Caillie

Auguste Rene Caillie was born on 19th November 1799 in Mauze, France, and he died on 17th May 1838 (aged 39 years) in France. Rene was the first modern European to have reached the cities of West Africa and to return alive from there. He decided to journey to Timbuktu despite not getting any financial backing. His knowledge of customs and language enabled him to travel there without any problem. He pretended to be an Egyptian Muslim pilgrim on reaching there. He made the detailed notes on the lifestyle, trade, buildings and people of the region.

Do you know: The Geographical Society of Paris awarded Rene a prize of 10,000 Franc for being the first traveller to visit and return from Timbuktu.

103. Francisco Vazquez de Coronado

Francisco Vazquez de Coronado was born in 1510 in Salamanca, Spain, and he died on 22nd September 1554 (aged 44 years) in Mexico City, Mexico. Francisco was known for the discovery of the Grand Canyon and various other landmarks in America. He started his expedition to find the fabled seven cities of gold as per the legend but became the first European to explore the American West. He sent his men in various directions to look for the gold cities and a group of them moved to Colorado where they were the first people to see the grand canyon.

Do you know: Francisco married the daughter of Alonso de Estrad who was a former colonial treasurer; because of this allaince he earned one of the largest estates in New Spain.

104. Caramuru

Caramuru or Diogo Alvares Correa was born in 1475 in Viana do Castelo, Portugal, and he died on 5th October 1557 (aged 82 years) in Salvador, Bahia, Brazil. A Portuguese settler who used his influence with the Indians to colonize Brazil, Caramuru went to Bahia to establish the settlement which came to be known as Vila Velha. He also assisted in founding Salvador and created the first governing body for Brazil. After his death Caramuru was buried in the Church of Jesus, and left half of his wealth to the Jesuits.

Do you know: Caramuru, the Tupi name was given to Diogo Alvares Correa by Tupinamba Indians after he was shipwrecked while sailing to the Portuguese colony in Brazil.

105. Joao Vaz Corte-Real

Joao Vaz Corte-Real was born in 1420 in Faro, Portugal, and he died in 1496 in Portugal. Known to have explored Terra Navo do Bacalhau which is a part of North America specifically Newfoundland, Joao was granted a part of Terceira because of his discovery. Joao Vaz Corte-Real was also granted the island of Sao Jorge where he tried to promote its settlement but couldn't achieve it. He and his wife, D Maria de Abarca were buried in the presbytery of the church of the Convent of Sao Francisco. His descendants did not live in the Capitania of Angra.

Do you know: The claim that he explored Terra Nova do Bacalhau originated from a book written by Gaspar Fructoses around 1570-80.

106. *Juan de la Cosa*

Juan de la Cosa was born in 1460 in Santona, Cantabria, Spain, and he died on 28th February 1510 (aged 50 years) in Turbaco, Columbia. Juan was a Spanish explorer and cartographer known for his voyages with Christopher Columbus in which they discovered America. In 1499, Juan made a voyage with Amerigo Vespucci and they explored the South American coast. He also explored Columbia and Panama along with two other famous explorers, Bastidas and Vasco Nunez de Balboa.

Do you know: Juan de la Cosa made a map of all the known lands of the New World called 'Mappa Mundi' which was the first officialy accepted map of the New World; it gave him considerable fame in Europe.

107. *Thomas Coulter*

Thomas Coulter was born in 1793 in Dundalk, Ireland and he died in 1843 (aged 50 years) in Dundalk, Ireland. Thomas was a botanist, physician and explorer who is remembered for his exploration and botanical research in Mexico, Arizona and California. The details and travels of his life are known only through fragmented records. He was a member of the Royal Irish Academy and was a renowned scholar of botany. Thomas was a physician with the Real Del Monte company in Mexico and it is during this time that he collected and studied the flora of this region. He studied botany in Geneva for seventeen months under Swiss taxonomist Augustin de Candolle.

Do you know: Thomas Coulter was a fellow of the Trinity College of Dublin where he founded the herbarium of the college.

108. *Thomas Crean*

Thomas Crean was born on 25th February 1877 in Annascaul, Ireland and he died on 27th July 1938 (aged 61 years) in Cork, Ireland. An Arctic explorer, Thomas was a member of three important expeditions to Antarctica including the one in which they lost the race to the South Pole to Roald Amundsen. He started his exploration career as a volunteer on the Discovery Expedition to Antarctica and his last exploration was with Ernest Shackleton's expedition.

Do you know: During the Terra Nova expedition Thomas Crean walked 56 km alone across the Ross Ice Shelf to save the life of Edward Evans and received the Albert Medal for Lifesaving.

109. *Tristao da Cunha*

Tristao da Cunha was born in 1460 in Portugal and he died in 1540 (aged 80 years) in Portugal. A naval commander and explorer, Tristao was the ambassador to the Pope Leo X. He led a fleet of 15 ships as commander to Africa and off India to take over the trade through the Red Sea and to take over Socotra Island and build a fortress there. During this voyage he discovered a group of remote Islands in the South Atlantic Ocean and named them after himself. After returning to Europe, Tristao was sent as an ambassador from King Manuel I to Pope Leo X in 1514 to present the new conquests of the Portuguese Empire.

Do you know: Tristao da Cunha was appointed the First Viceroy of Portuguese India but could not take up the post due to temporary blindness that afflicted him.

110. *Jeremy Curl*

Jeremy Curl was born on 13th March 1982 in Tokyo, Japan, and he still lives today. He resides in London, England. Jeremy is a photographer and filmmaker who has travelled widely in Africa and Asia. He was the first non-African to cross the Tanezrouft area of the Sahara without a motorized transport. He lived and travelled with the nomad tribe of the region. While in Sahara he crossed 1200 miles on foot and by camel starting from Hoggar Mountains to Timbuktu in Mali in 50 days. He spent time in an unrecognized country of Transnistria and came out with pictures never seen before.

Do you know: Jeremy Curl carried out an expedition across the Danakali Depression, the 'Cruellest place on the Earth' with temperatures up to 60 degrees.

111. *William Healy Dall*

William Healy Dall was born on 21st August, 1845 in Boston, USA, and he died on 27th March 1927 (aged 81 years) in Washington DC, USA. William was a naturalist, malacologist and one of the first people to scientifically explore the interiors of Alaska. He undertook his first expedition with Robert Kennicott as his assistant. He explored the coast of Siberia and stopped several times in Alaska. William took over the expedition after Kennicott's death and decided to take on the exploration of the flora and fauna of the unchartered area of Alaska after it was taken over by America. He collected thousands of specimens from there, catalogued and described them.

Do you know: William Healy Dall has numerous species named after him. These species include mammals, plants and invertebrates.

112. *William Dampier*

William Dampier was born on 5th September 1651 in Somerset, England, and he died in March 1715 (aged 64 years). William Dampier was the first European to explore Australia and the first person to circumnavigate the world thrice. He wrote an account of his travels in four volumes entitled 'New Voyage Round the World' which became hugely popular. Also, his account of the winds and current of the Pacific in his second volume has the navigators and meteorologists of the present day impressed. William Dampier had reached Australia on one of his voyages but he took a dislike to it and its people and their customs.

Do you know: William's naval service was cut short due to an illness and later he tried his hand at several careers such as plantation management in Jamaica, logging in Mexico, etc.

113. *Aloha Wanderwell*

Aloha Wanderwell was born on 13th October 1906 in Winniepeg, Canada, and she died on 4th June 1996 (aged 90 years) in Newport Beach, California. Aloha was an explorer, author and film-maker. She holds a Guinness World Record for being the 'first female to drive around the world'. She travelled to 43 countries starting and ending in Nice, France in a Ford Model T. During the expedition she encountered the first aerial circumnavigators in Calcutta in 1924 and recorded their meeting. During an expedition to Brazil Aloha made the first contact with the Bororo people and also made a film about it.

Do you know: Aloha Wanderwell travelled to 80 countries in all, covering 5,00,000 miles, all in Fords.

114. *Adrien de Gerlache*

Adrien de Gerlache was born on 2nd August 1866 in Hasselt, Belgium, and he died on 4th December 1934 (aged 67 years) in Brussels, Belgium. Adrien was a Belgian naval officer who led the Belgian Antarctic Expedition of 1897-99. He decided to voyage to Antarctica for which he purchased his own ship. After sailing through, charting and naming a string of Islands they crossed the Antarctic Circle. They got stranded in the Bellinghausen Sea getting trapped in ice and had to spend over seven months trying to get it out. He also sailed to the Persian Gulf, Greenland Sea and a few other expeditions over the years.

Do you know: Adrien de Gerlache wrote a book about the expedition and was awarded a prize by the Academie Francaise.

115. *Pierre-Jean De Smet*

Pierre-Jean De Smet was born on 30th January 1801 in Dendermonde, Belgium, and he died on 23rd May 1873 (aged 72 years) in Saint Louis, Missouri, United States. Pierre-Jean was a Belgian Catholic priest and is known for his extensive travels as a missionary in Western and Mid-western North America as well as western Canada in the mid-19th century. He produced the first detailed map of the Missouri river valley. It shows the locations of the native Villages and other cultural features along with the physical features of the area. He undertook the Canadian Rockies Expedition which was the longest explorations that he undertook.

Do you know: Pierre-Jean remained active in missionary work till his death and raised money for several missions.

116. *Semyon Dezhnev*

Semyon Dezhnev was born in 7th March 1605 in Veliky Ustyug, Russia and he died in 1673 (aged 68 years) in Moscow, Russia. Semyon was a Russian explorer of Siberia and the first European to sail into the Bering Strait much before Vitus Bering. He travelled to Siberia on an expedition organized in an attempt to reach the area near the Arctic. They attempted to move to an area near Pogycha River which failed twice before they reached it. They were shipwrecked and stranded there for almost a year. They had sailed from Kolyma River on the Arctic ocean to Anadyr river on the Pacific ocean.

Do you know: Semyon Dezhnev did not lay claim to his discovery of Bering Strait, hence, it was forgotten for about a hundred years and Bering was given the credit for discovering it.

117. *Karl Von Ditmar*

Karl Von Ditmar was born 8th September 1822 in Vandra, Estonia, and he died on 25th April 1892 (aged 70 years) in Tartu, Estonia. A geologist and explorer best known to have travelled and given a scientific explanation and understanding of Kamchatka, which is in the far east of Russia. He undertook a voyage to Kamchatka peninsula and stayed there till 1854. He undertook important scientific investigations to study the area which includes volcanoes, rivers as well as mountains. He published his works in 1890 and it is still referred to by scientists involved in the study of this region.

Do you know: Karl von Ditmar was a Baltic German who contributed to the scientific understanding of the Kamchatka which is now a UNESCO heritage site.

118. *Gil Eanes*

Gil Eanes was born in 1395 in Laos Portugal and he died in 1445. A Portuguese and explorer, Gil is known to be the first person to sail beyond the Cape Bojador which was then considered impassable. He failed in the first exploration attempt to go round Cape Bojador as he drifted towards Canary islands from where he captured some natives and brought them back. He succeeded in the following year and reported on the weather, water and the way to navigate beyond the Cape. This enabled the extensive Portuguese Exploration of Africa.

Do you know: Very little is known about the life of Gil Eanes before he undertook the voyages beyond Cape Bojador. He is said to have been the household servant and a shield bearer for Henry, the navigator.

119. *Juan Sebastian Elcano*

Juan Sebastian Elcano was born in 1476 in Getaria, Gipuzkoa, Spain, and he died on 4th August 1526 (aged 50 years) at the Pacific ocean. Juan Sebastian was a mariner, navigator and explorer. He is credited with doing the first circumnavigation of the Earth. He led a mutiny against Magellan who was in charge. During this voyage they discovered a passage, now known as Strait of Magellan, near the southern tip of South America. They set sail for the Pacific ocean after their crew had mutinied and returned to Spain. They finally reached Moluccas and they continued westwards crossing the Indian and Atlantic oceans.

Do you know: Juan Sebastian Elcano's expedition covered 81,449 km and only 17 of the 240 crew members returned.

120. *George Everest*

Sir George Everest was born on 4th July 1790 in Wales, United Kingdom and he died on 1st December 1866 (aged 76 years) in Hyde Park Gardens, London, United Kingdom. Sir George was a geographer and surveyor who became well known for exploring much of India and Nepal. He was the Surveyor-General of India where he commanded all the geological and surveying missions. After he had retired and moved back to England, he served in prestigious positions with Royal Society and Royal Geographical Society. He was knighted in 1861 in recognition for all his work.

Do you know: Mount Everest was named after Sir George in his honour, although it was never surveyed by him.

121. *Evliya Celebi*

Mehmed Zilli, known as Evliya Celebi, was born on 25th March 1611 (aged 71 years) in Constantinople, Ottoman Empire, and he died on 1682 in Cairo, Egypt. Evliya was an Ottoman explorer who over a period of forty years travelled the Ottoman Empire and the areas around it. He is known to have travelled to Austria, Hungary, Iraq, Iran, Sudan, Syria, Palestine, Azerbaijan, Crimea and Greece. He wrote about his travels extensively in a book entitled 'Seyahatname' which means Travelogue. He has described the bridge in Mostar, the Parthenon and has described the political situations, the architecture and the local culture and customs.

Do you know: Evliya has collected the specimen of each and every language in each region he travelled.

122. *Ahmad ibn Fadlan*

Ahmad ibn Fadlan was born in 877 AD in Baghdad, Iraq, and he died in 960 AD (aged 83 years). Ahmad was an Arab traveller known for his writing about his travels as an Embassy member of Baghdad to the King of Volga Bulgars, now in Russia. He called his book 'Risala'. He provided very detailed descriptions of the Volga Vikings. Ahmad was with the party in the capacity of the religious advisor for Islamic law. The delegation covered about 4,000 km through Bukhara, now Uzbekistan and through the regions of the Caspian and Ural rivers, giving the account of the people there.

Do you know: Ahmad thought of the Bulgar people and described them as perfect physical specimens, tall and blond with ruddy complexions but found their sense of hygiene disgusting.

123. *Percy Fawcett*

Lieutenant Colonel Percy Harrison Fawcett was born on 18th August 1867 in Torquay, United Kingdom, and he died on 29th May 1925 (aged 58 years) in Mato Grosso, Brazil. An artillery officer, archaeologist and explorer, Percy is best known for exploring South America when he was trying to look for the lost city of El Dorado in the jungles of Brazil. His first ever expedition to South America was to map the jungle area between Brazil and Bolivia for the Royal Geographical Society. He made seven expeditions between the years 1906 and 1924. On his last expedition, he set out with his eldest son and his friend to find the lost city which he called 'Z'.

Do you know: Sir Arthur Conan Doyle used Fawcett's reports of the Amazonian region as an inspiration for his novel 'The Lost World'.

124. *Salvador Fidalgo*

Salvador Fidalgo was born on 6th August 1756 in Spain and he died on 27th September 1803 (aged 47 years) in Tacubaya, Mexico City, Mexico. Salvador was a Spanish explorer who commanded an expedition for Spain to Alaska and the Pacific Northwest during the 18th century. He was a member of the team of cartographers who were working on the first atlas of Spain's coasts and waters. Salvador was sent to Spain's furthermost settlement just off today's Vancouver Island. He sailed and anchored in the present day Alaska and claimed it for the Spanish sovereignty. He sailed further ahead and discovered a port they decided to call 'Puerto Valdez'.

Do you know: In 1778, Salvador Fidalgo was assigned to the Spanish naval station at San Blas, Mexico.

125. *Mattew Flinders*

Captain Mattew Flinders was born on 16th March 1774 in Donington, United Kingdom, and he died on 19th July 1814 (aged 40 years) in London, England. Mattew was an English cartographer and navigator who was the leader of the expedition which took the first circumnavigation of Australia and recognized it as a continent. Mattew undertook three voyages to the oceans in the South. It is in the third voyage that he circumnavigated the mainland with an aboriginal man called Bungaree. He decided to call the entire landmass 'Australia'.

Do you know: Mattew wrote a full account of his voyage and an atlas for publication which he called 'A Voyage to Terra Australis'. He died a day after the book and the atlas were published at the age of 40.

126. *Peter Forsskal*

Peter Forsskal was born on 11th January 1732 in Helsinki, Finland, and he died on 11th July 1763 (aged 31 years) in Yemen. A naturalist and an orientalist, Peter studied theology and was a disciple of Linnaeus, who was a renowned botanist. Peter published a political paper on Civil Liberty and advocated the complete freedom of print which was controversial for those times. He was appointed to join an expedition to Arabia where they stayed in Egypt for a year. He studied Arabic dialect and arrived in the present day Yemen where he worked hard in collecting numerous botanical and zoological specimens.

Do you know: One of the plant species Peter Forsskal had sent home was named after him because the plant was as stubborn and persistent as the young Forsskal had been.

127. *John Franklin*

Sir John Franklin was born on 16th April 1786 in Spilsby, United Kingdom, and he died on 11th June 1847 (aged 61 years) in King William Island, Canada. Franklin entered the Royal Navy at the age of 14, accompanied Matthew Flinders on his exploratory voyage to Australia, and served in the Battles of Trafalgar and New Orleans. A naval officer and explorer of the Arctic, Sir John went in search for the North-west Passage. He charted the north coast of Canada and took a voyage to the Arctic. In his second voyage, he wanted to explore the 500 km left unchartered but the crew disappeared on this expedition and were not heard again despite numerous searches.

Do you know: Sir John Franklin was named the Governor of Tasmania, knighted and awarded the Gold Medal by Geographical Society of France.

128. *Simon Fraser II*

Simon Fraser II was born on 20th May 1776 in Hoosick, Province of New York, British America, and he died on 18th August 1862 (aged 86 years) in Saint. Andrews West, Canada. Simon was an explorer who has explored and chartered most of the British Columbia region of Canada. He is also credited with establishing the first ever European settlement in British Columbia. He discovered and explored a river which now bears his name 'Fraser River'. He was a fur trader by trade, a job in which he was very successful and became a full partner in his company by the age of 25. In this capacity, he established various trading posts and explored new areas to extend their trade route.

Do you know: Simon Fraser II was offered a Knighthood but declined due to his limited wealth.

129. *John C Fremont*

John Charles Fremont was born on 21st January 1813 in Savannah, Georgia, United States, and he died on 13th July 1890 (aged 77 years) in New York. A politician who undertook expeditions to the American West and was called the 'Path Finder', John mapped the second half of the Oregon Trail. The third expedition led to the source of the Arkansas river. As his final expedition, he also led a expedition seeking a rail route over the mountains around the 38th parallel latitude which was very arduous.

Do you know: John Charles Fremont was the first Presidential candidate of the Anti-Slavery Republican Party; he stood for the office of the President of the United States.

130. *Xu Fu*

Xu Fu was born in 255 BC, in Qi, ancient China. Xu Fu was a court sorcerer and was sent on two voyages to look for the Elixir of Life by Qin Shi Huang, the ruler of Qin. Xu travelled for many years with a fleet of 60 ships, 5000 crew members and various artisans and three thousand boys and girls. It is said that he landed in Japan and named Mount Fuji as Penglai. He is said to have been instrumental in the development of the ancient Japanese culture and society. Xu introduced new farming techniques and knowledge in agriculture and it is believed that he introduced many new plants to the Japanese.

Do you know: Xu Fu is worshipped as the god of silk, farming and Medicine by the Japanese and there are numerous temples dedicated to him in many places in Japan.

131. *Louis Claude de Freycinet*

Louis Claude de Freycinet was born on 7th August 1779 in Drome, France, and he died on 18th August 1841 (aged 62 years) in France. Louis was a French navigator, cartographer and explorer who circumnavigated the Earth and he is attributed with making the first map to show the full outline of Australia. He had set out to explore the coasts of Australia and covered much of the area previously discovered by Mattew Flinders. He undertook the circumnavigation of the Earth with the aim of collecting not only geographical data but also data in astronomy and meteorology and natural history.

Do you know: Louis Claude de Freycinet managed to get his wife Rose aboard the ship Uranie, disguised as a man. She was the first woman to record her experience of circumnavigating the world.

132. *Nellie Bly*

Elizabeth Jane Cochran, well known as Nellie Bly, was born on 5th May 1864 in Cochran's Mills, Pennsylvania, United States, and she died of pneumonia on 22nd January 1922 (aged 57 years) in New York City. Nellie was an American journalist who set the world record for the fastest trip around the world. Inspired by Jules Verne, she completed the journey from England, through Europe, Asia and onwards to North America in 72 days. She was the first woman to drive across India as well as Cape Town to the Nile. In 1895, Nellie married millionarie industrialist Robert Seaman, and subsequently became legally known as Elizabeth Jane Cochrane Seaman.

Do you know: Nellie Bly received patents for several inventions including a stacking garbage can and an innovative milk can.

133. *Vivian Fuchs*

Sir Vivian Ernest Fuchs was born on 11th February 1908 in Freshwater, United Kingdom, and he died on 11th November 1999 (aged 91 years) in Cambridge, United Kingdom. Sir Vivian was a geologist and explorer who made his name by completing the first crossing of Antarctica over the land in 1958. They completed this feat in a 100 days by travelling 2,158 miles. They collected valuable data along the way. Sir Vivian's team established that there was landmass underneath the ice and measured the thickness of ice at the Poles. Vivian Ernest Fuchs also made expeditions to study the geology of East African lakes in climatic terms and an expedition to Olduvai Gorge.

Do you know: The Fuchs Medal was created in 1973 and is awarded to one or two people per year for their contribution to the British Antarctic Survey.

134. *Dionisio Alcala Galiano*

Dionisio Alcala Galiano was born on 8th October 1760 in Cabra, Spain, and he died on 21st October 1805 (aged 45 years) in Cape Trafalgar, Spain. A cartographer, naval officer and explorer, Dionisio led an expedition that mapped the Strait of Juan de Fuca and the Strait of Georgia. He was also the first European to circumnavigate the Vancouver Island. He explored and accurately mapped the numerous coastlines of Europe and the Americas using new technology such as chronometers. He sailed with Malaspina in a scientific and political voyage as a hydrographer.

Do you know: Dionisio Alcala Galiano who was then a brigadier fought in the battle of Trafalgar where he was killed by a cannonball.

135. *Pedro Sarmiento de Gamboa*

Pedro Sarmiento de Gamboa was born in 1532 in Galicia, Spain, and he died in 1592 (aged 60 years) Lisbon, Portugal. A Spanish explorer, author, historian, mathematician, astronomer and scientist, Pedro Sarmiento started by sailing across the Atlantic Ocean to Mexico. He lived there for two years before moving on to Peru where he lived for two decades. He wrote a very detailed account of the Inca history and mythology. Pedro joined Alvaro de Mendana in looking for Australia but instead discovered the Solomon Islands.

Do you know: Alvaro threw away Pedro's journals and maps and abandoned him in Mexico to take credit for the discovery but after a trial Pedro was given his due credit.

136. *Thomas Gann*

Thomas William Francis Gann was born on 13th May 1867 in Murrisk Abbey, Ireland, and he died on 24th February 1938 (aged 71 years) in London, UK. A doctor by profession but Thomas is best known for his exploration as an amateur archaeologist of the Mayan civilization ruins. He was stationed in British Honduras as a medical officer where he got interested in the ruins of the Mayan Civilisation in the colony. He explored and documented all the buildings which included a rare temple with an idol intact inside it. He discovered numerous sites which include Lubaantun, Ichpaatun and Tzibanche.

Do you know: Thomas Gann wrote several books about his travels and sold a large number of objects he had collected from the Mayan ruins to the British museum.

137. *Francis Garnier*

Marie Joseph Francis Garnier was born on 25th July 1839 in Saint Etienne, France, and he died on 21st December 1873 (aged 34 years) in Hanoi, Vietnam. Francis was a French officer and became famous for being the person to conceive the idea and to explore the valley of the Mekong River region. He undertook the major work of surveying and observing the positions fixed by astronomical observations in the area which was unknown to the Europeans exploring the area. Francis assumed command of the expedition after the leader Lagree had died. He wrote an anonymous account of his experiences during the siege; his experiences were published later on.

Do you know: Francis Garnier took over Hanoi, died in that battle and was later awarded for his feat of bravery.

138. *Romolo Gessi*

Romolo Gessi was born on 30th April 1831 in Ravenna, Italy, and he died on 1st May 1881 (aged 50 years) in Suez, Egypt. Romolo was an Italian soldier and explorer who is well-known for having explored North-east Africa, especially Sudan and the Nile River. He fought with the British forces in the Crimean war where he first met General Charles Gordon. He invited Romolo to accompany him to Sudan. There he participated in the exploration of the Upper Nile. He was also the first person to circumnavigate Lake Albert and map its descent. He also conducted the explorations of the interiors of Sudan.

Do you know: Romolo suppressed a revolt of the Arab traders there. For this service rendered by him, he was given the title of Pasha, by the Khedive of Egypt and came to be known as Gessi Pasha.

139. *Ernest Giles*

William Ernest Powell Giles was born on 20th July 1835 in Bristol, England, and he died on 13th November 1897 (aged 62 years) in Coolgardie, Australia. William was an Australian explorer who led five expeditions in central Australia. He first explored north-west of Darling River looking for pastoral and cultivable land for hemp. On his second expedition, with two other men he explored the unchartered territory around Lake Amadeus. He was also the first person to see the rock formations called Kata Tjuta. He made three more expeditions to the interiors of Australia. He published two books describing his five explorations.

Do you know: Ernest Giles named the desert 'Gibson Desert' after his companion who died enroute.

140. *James Augustus Grant*

James Augustus Grant was born on 11th April 1827 in Nairn, United Kingdom, and he died on 11th February 1892 (aged 64 years) in Nairn, United Kingdom. An explorer, author and armed forces officer, James explored the eastern equatorial Africa. He joined the Indian army and served during the Indian mutiny of 1857. He later returned to England and joined John Speke in the Nile expedition. James collected valuable specimens for botanical studies and carried out independent investigations. He published an account of the journey in which he described the everyday life and habits of the natives. He also served in the intelligence department of the Abyssinian expedition.

Do you know: James Augustus Grant joined the Indian army and served during the Indian mutiny of 1857.

141. *Juan de Grijalva*

Juan de Grijalva was born around 1489 in Cuellar, Spain, and he died on 21st January 1527 (aged 38 years) in Nicaragua. Juan was one of the earliest people to explore the shores of Mexico. He accompanied Velaquez when he voyaged to Cuba. Velaquez sent Juan to explore the Yucatan Peninsula and after rounding the Guaniguanico in Cuba, he sailed along the coast of Mexico and discovered Cozumel. The Rio Grijalva in Mexico was named after him. He was also the first Spaniard to learn of the existence of the Aztec empire farther North. He also accompanied Cortes on his expedition the basis of which was his earlier exploration of Mexico. He was killed by natives in Honduras.

Do you know: Juan de Grijalva was the nephew of Diego Velazquez, another famous explorer. Hernan Cortes, a Spanish explorer, also stayed at Grijalva's home in Trinidad, Cuba.

142. *Ahmed Hassanein*

Ahmed Hassanein Pasha was born on 31st October 1889 in Cairo, Egypt, and he died on 19th February 1946 (aged 57 years) Cairo, Egypt. An Egyptian courtier and was also a writer, photographer and explorer, Ahmed discovered unknown water sources on his journey to Kufra which resulted in the making of new routes to Sudanic Africa. During this expedition he took photographs, samples, measured distances and took bearing and wrote in his diary about the traditions and the natural history enroute. He is also credited with writing the history and traditions of fierce and hostile tribe of Senissis in Libya. His pictures were published in the National Geographic Magazine.

Do you know: Ahmed Hassanein Pasha was an Olympic athlete. He competed at the 1920 and 1924 Olympics in Fencing.

143. *Ferdinand Vandeveer Hayden*

Ferdinand Vandeveer Hayden was born on 7th September 1829 in Massachusetts, USA, and he died on 22nd December 1887 (aged 58 years) in Philadelphia, USA. A physician and geologist known for pioneering survey expeditions of the Rocky Mountains in the later part of the 19th century, Ferdinand organized and headed geographic surveys to Nebraska and western territories for the US Government. His dozen years of surveying gave valuable data in the branches of natural history and economic sciences. He also published an atlas on the geography and geology of Colorado.

Do you know: Ferdinand Vandeveer Hayden uncovered and collected numerous dinosaur-fossils during his extensive geological surveys which added much to the study of dinosaurs.

144. *Sven Hedin*

Sven Anders Hedin was born on 19th February 1865 in Stockholm, Sweden, and he died on 26th November 1952 (aged 87 years) in Stockholm, Sweden. A Swedish explorer, writer and topographer, Sven is noted for locating the sources of the Brahmaputra, Indus and Sutlej Rivers. He made daring expeditions into Central Asia where he mapped and explored the parts of China and Tibet. His notes were valuable in the accurate mapping of Central Asia. He conducted a Trans-Himalayan expedition and was the first European to reach the sacred Lake Mansarovar and Mount Kailash.

Do you know: Sven Anders Hedin wrote adventure stories for young readers which made him famous.

145. *Matthew Henson*

Matthew Henson was born on 8th August 1866 in Maryland, United States, and he died on 9th March 1955 (aged 89 years) in New York, United States. The first African-American explorer, Matthew was the co-discoverer of the North Pole along with Robert Edwin Peary. He made an expedition to Nicaragua and Greenland learning the language and skills of the Inuits, also collecting meteorites they had found in their previous trips and sold them to fund their next expedition.

Do you know: Matthew Henson remained overlooked due to being an African-American and finally received recognition at the age of 70 when the Explorers Club of New York gave him honorary membership.

146. *Louis Hennepin*

Louis Hennepin was born on 12th May 1626 in the present day Belgium and he died on 5th December 1704 (aged 78 years) in Rome. Louis was a Roman Catholic priest who was a missionary and an explorer of the interiors of North America. He was sent to sail through the Great Lakes and explore the unknown West. They reached somewhere near the present Illinois and Louis was sent further to search for River Mississippi. He brought forth the existence of the Niagara Falls, and the Saint Anthony Falls, the only Falls on the Mississippi.

Do you know: Louis Hennepin's claim of discovering the Mississippi is untrue as he claimed to have found it two years before LaSalle, who was the leader of the expedition.

147. *William Lewis Herndon*

Commander William Lewis Herndon was born on 25th October 1813, Virginia, USA, and he died on 12th September 1857 (aged 44 years), North Carolina, USA. A naval officer and explorer, William is well-known for his exploration of the Valley of Amazon which was mostly unknown at that time. He worked his way treading 4,336 miles exploring the main river and its tributaries through thick forests to the heights of over 16,000 ft. He made a detailed report which was published and widely circulated and cited in the future works of natural history and ethnology of other people.

Do you know: William saved 152 women and children when the ship they were sailing in got sunk; they chose to remain with 400 others who perished. This was one of the biggest tragedies in the history of the US.

148. *Clement Hodgkinson*

Clement Hodgkinson was born in 1818, South Hampton, UK, and he died on 5th September 1893 (aged 75 years) Melbourne, Australia. A naturalist and surveyor, Clement explored the northeastern areas of New South Wales becoming the first European to come in contact with the Aborigines. He then went on to follow the river valleys of the rivers in that region which included the Hastings, Tweed, Richmond and the Clarence. He then visited Brisbane and Port Macquarie and Moreton Bay. He later published his account of the travel wherein he mentioned about the life and the natural history of the Aborigines. Hodgkinsonia ovatiflora, commonly referred to as Hodgkinsonia or Golden ash, was named after Clement Hodgkinson.

Do you know: St Vincent Garden in Albert Park, which is now a nationally significant park, was designed by Clement.

149. *Emil Holub*

Emil Holub was born on 7th October 1847 in Holice, Czech Republic, and he died on 21st February 1902 (aged 55 years) in Vienna, Austria. A Czech physician and cartographer, Emil was inspired by the writing of David Livingstone and settled in Kimberely in South Africa to practise medicine. His first expedition was experimental where he collected a large number of the specimen of natural history. He made the first ever map of the region around the Victoria Falls. He attempted to explore the entire length of Africa from Cape Town to Egypt but the expedition could not be completed.

Do you know: Emil Holub, unable to find a home for his artefacts, gradually sold or gave away parts of it to museums and scientific institutes as well as schools.

150. *William Hovell*

William Hilton Hovell was born on 26th April 1786 in Great Yarmouth, United Kingdom, and he died on 9th November 1875 (aged 89 years) in Sydney, Australia. William is known for exploring Australia along with Hamilton Hume; they are credited with exploring much of Victoria. He discovered the Burragorang valley. He and Hamilton Hume were asked to explore the southern part of New South Wales to know about any rivers that might run through that area. Governor Ralph Darling sent a ship to have it explored and William discovered coal in Victoria. This turned out to be an important discovery.

Do you know: Hamilton Hume and William Hovell feuded till their death over taking credit for their discoveries of Victoria.

151. *Alexander von Humboldt*

Friedrich Wilhelm Heinrich Alexander von Humboldt was born on 14th September 1769 in Berlin, Germany, and he died on 6th May 1859 (aged 89 years) in Berlin, Germany. A Prussian geographer, Alexander explored Latin America and described it for the first time scientifically, laying the foundation of modern geomagnetic and meteorological monitoring. He was one of the first people to propose that the land bordering the Atlantic Ocean, South America and Africa, was once joined. Between 1799 and 1804, he travelled extensively in Latin America, exploring and describing it for the first time from a modern scientific point of view.

Do you know: Alexander von Humboldt while working in the Department of Mines opened free school for miners and established relief fund for miners.

152. *Hamilton Hume*

Hamilton Hume was born on 19th June 1797 in Seven Hills, Australia, and he died on 19th April 1873 (aged 76 years), Yass, Australia. An explorer of the present day Australian states of New South Wales and Victoria, Hamilton was an expert Bushman. He went on the journey with the Surveyor-General and another person during which Lake Bathurst and Goulburn Plains were discovered. He is most well-known for the expedition he undertook along with William Hilton Hovell to explore the area from Sydney to Port Philip. Hamilton and the expedition team were the first Europeans to discover the Darling River, the longest tributary of the Murray River.

Do you know: Hamilton incorrectly thought that Hovell had taken credit for discovering Victoria and feuded with him till death.

153. *James S Hutchinson*

James Sather Hutchinson was born on 1867 in San Francisco, California, USA, and he died on 1959 (aged 92 years). A lawyer, mountaineer and environmentalist, James is noted for exploring Sierra Nevada. He along with Le Conte and Mc Duffie pioneered a high mountain route from Yosemite National Park to King's Canyon. They had covered 228 miles in 28 days. He also was the first to lead an expedition from Giant Forest to Roaring River country over the Colby Pass. He as a mountaineer had climbed numerous mountains including Mount Humphrey, Mount Abbot and Mount Sill and many more.

Do you know: James Sather Hutchinson's career as a lawyer lasted 60 years and he attended court on his 90th birthday.

154. *Helge Ingstad*

Helge Marcus Ingstad was born on 30th December 1899 in Meraker, Norway, and he died on 29th March 2001 (aged 101 years) in Oslo, Norway. Helge was a Norwegian explorer who not only mapped the Norse settlements but also found the remains of a Viking settlement in New Foundland, Canada. He and his wife, who was an archaeologist, went on to prove with this finding that the Norsemen were crossing the Atlantic Ocean to get to North America much before Christopher Columbus or John Cabot. It is the only site of a Norse settlement in Canada and North America except Greenland. This might have had a connection to Leif Eriksson's settlement of Vinland.

Do you know: Helge was a famous author in Norway and wrote about his travels to remote places.

155. *Roberto Ivens*

Roberto Ivens was born on 12th June 1850 in Ponta Delgada, Portugal, and he died on 28th January 1898 (aged 47 years) in Lisbon, Portugal. Roberto was an explorer, geographer and naval officer who is famed for the exploration of Africa. He began his exploration in Angola and for three years travelled the colonies of Portugal in Africa. While on the expedition to Angola and Mozambique he studied the hydrography of the basins of Zambezi. This study of his is considered perfect even today. His travels between these two countries finished covering over 4,500 miles and one-third of that area was unexplored.

Do you know: Roberto Ivens also travelled to the United States carrying Portuguese goods for the Centennial Exposition. He was the great grandson of Thomas Hickling.

156. *Thorfinn Karlsefni*

Thorfinn Karlsefni was born around the year 980 AD in Iceland and he died after 1007 AD. Following the footsteps of Leif Eriksson, Thorfinn made his way to Vinland in an attempt to establish a permanent colony there. His expeditions are known because of their mention in the 'Saga of the Greenlanders' and the 'Saga of Erik the Red'. Thorfinn is said to have decided to go to Vinland on the insistence of Gudrid, his wife. He took three ships and about 140 men with him and some women with them including his wife. The location of the colony is assumed to be L'Anse aux Meadows in Newfoundland, Canada.

Do you know: Thorfinn and Gudrid's son Snorri is said to be the first child of European descent to be born in the New World.

157. Johann Karl Ehrenfried Kegel

Johann Karl Ehrenfried Kegel was born on 3rd October 1784 in Friesdorf, Germany, and he died on 25th June 1863 (aged 79 years) in Odessa, Ukraine. Known as the explorer of Kamchatka Peninsula, Johann was sent to Kamchatka by the Russian Government to check it for the possibilities of agriculture and mining. He travelled through Siberia and arrived in Kamchatka, shipwrecked. He made arduous journeys into the heart of the land. He wrote very detailed accounts of the flora and fauna of the area. He also mentions the soil and geology of the area. Johann also discovered the mineral resources and saw the potential of the area.

Do you know: Johann was victimized by the corrupt local politician who did not allow him to publish his report.

158. George Kennan

George Kennan was born on 16th February 1845 in Norwalk, Ohio, United States, and he died on 10th May 1924 (aged 79 years) in Medina, New York, United States. George was a journalist and American explorer who is known for his travels to Kamchatka and Caucasus regions of the Russian Empire. George travelled to Russia for the first time when he was sent there by his company to survey the area for a proposed telegraph line through Siberia. Later, he travelled to the Caucasus region and became the first American to explore its highlands and write about the herders, silversmiths, carpet weavers and other craftsmen of the remote region.

Do you know: George Kennan spent 20 years lecturing against the Imperialist Russian rule and published the first English language journal that opposed the Tsarist Russia.

159. Edmund Kennedy

Edmund Besley Court Kennedy was born on 5th September 1818 in Guernsey, United Kingdom, and he died on 23 December 1848 (aged 30 years) in Cape York Peninsula, Queensland, Australia. An English explorer in Australia, Edmund Kennedy explored the interiors of Queensland and northern New South Wales which included the Thomson and Barcoo Rivers, Cooper Creek and Cape York Peninsula. He encountered terrible terrains and travelled only 40 miles in more than two months. Only three people survived the expedition. In 1847, Edmund discovered that the Victoria River did not flow into the Gulf as Mitchell thought, but was part of Coopers Creek. He renamed it the Barcoo River.

Do you know: Edmund Kennedy was killed by the natives and he died in the arms of his aboriginal Guide Jackey Jackey.

160. Robert Kennicott

Robert Kennicott was born on 13th November 1835 in New Orleans, Louisiana, United States, and he died on 13th May 1866 (aged 31 years) in Alaska, United States. A naturalist, Robert undertook an expedition to Northwestern Canada to collect natural history specimens in the Sub-Arctic boreal forests which are now Mackenzie and Yukon River valleys. Illinois was still unexplored and he sent many samples from that area. He died during this trip in the Yukon area. He advocated for the study and protection of native prairie animals in an era when farmers sought to eradicate them.

Do you know: Robert due to a chronic illness stayed out of school most of his childhood but got a good education at home.

161. Eusebio Kino

Eusebio Francisco Kino was born on 10th August 1645 in the Holy Roman Empire and he died on 15th March 1711 (aged 66 years) in the Spanish Empire. An Italian Jesuit, geographer, cartographer and explorer, Eusebio was a missionary who stayed in the region which is now Sonora in Mexico and southern Arizona in the United States. He proved that the Baja California Peninsula is not an island by leading an expedition over land. Eusebio travelled across northern Mexico following the established trading routes. His many expeditions covered an area of 50,000 sq.miles while he mapped an area which was 320 km long and 400 km wide.

Do you know: Eusebio opposed slavery and compulsory hard labour in the silver mines that the natives were forced to do.

162. Maria Klenova

Maria Vasilyevna Klenova was born in 12th August 1898, in Irkutsk, Russia, and she died on 6th August 1976 (aged 78 years) in Moscow, Russia. Maria was a Russian marine geologist and contributor to the first Soviet Antarctic atlas which was groundbreaking work. She made the first complete sea bed map of the Barents Sea and was also one of the founders of Russian marine science. She has the claim of being the first woman scientist to do research in Antarctica. She spent nearly 30 years researching the Polar Regions. She travelled with the Russian oceanographic team to map the unexplored areas of the Antarctic coast.

Do you know: An oceanographic valley, a crater on Venus and a peak in Antarctica are all named after her.

163. *Amyr Klink*

Amyr Klink was born on 25th September 1955 in Sao Paulo, Brazil, and he still lives today. Amyr was a sailor and explorer who is best known for circumnavigating Antarctic continent on his own in 79 days in 1998. Amyr was also the first person to row across the South Atlantic starting from Namibia and reach to Salvador, Brazil, in a 100 days. In this expedition, he rowed the boat with his hands. His other achievement has been to take a trip around the world through a maritime path, the Arctic Circle, that had never been explored before. This was an experimental part of a project he had undertaken. He has written seven books about his voyages.

Do you know: Amyr bought his first boat at the age of 10 and his collection has exceeded 30 in number.

164. *Alexander Kolchak*

Alexander Vasilyevich Kolchak was born on 16th November 1874 in Saint Petersburg, Russia, and he died on 7th February 1920 (aged 46 years) in Irkutsk, Soviet Russia. A commander in the Imperial Russian Navy and Polar explorer, Alexander helped design two special ice breakers to be launched for a cartographic expedition. He commanded one of these vessels during these expeditions and collected material for research. He received the highest award of the Russian Geographical Society for his exploration and he came to be known as 'Kolchak the Polar'.

Do you know: Alexander Kolchak established an anti-communist government in Siberia and for a year and a half, he was internationally recognized as the leader of Russia.

165. *Fyodor Konyukhov*

Fyodor Konyukhov (Fedor Filippovich Konyukhov) was born on 12th December 1951 in the village of Chkalovo, Ukraine, and he still lives today. A Russian survivalist, sailor and balloon pilot, Fyodor is the only person to have reached the extreme points on the planets, the North Pole (thrice), the South Pole, Pole of inaccessibility in the Arctic Ocean and twice on top of Mount Everest. He completed a solo circumnavigation of Antarctica in a sailboat, the first person to do so. He has set world records in rowing such as rowing across the Atlantic Ocean in 46 days and going a distance of 110 miles in 24 hours.

Do you know: Fyodor has been the second person to circumnavigate the world in a hot-air helium balloon on 23rd July 2016.

166. *Otto von Kotzebue*

Otto von Kotzebue was born on 30th December 1787 in Reval, now in Tallinn, Estonia, and he died on 15th February 1846 (aged 58 years) in Tallinn, Estonia. A Russian naval officer who circumnavigated the Earth three times, Otto charted much of the Alaskan coast and commanded an expedition to find a passage across the Arctic Ocean and explore the lesser known parts of Oceania. During this voyage he discovered the Romanzov Islands, Rurik Islands and Krusenstern Islands which he discovered in the remote Chukchi Sea. In his second expedition, with a staff of scientists he collected valuable information in geography, ethnography and natural history.

Do you know: Otto was the son of a famous German dramatist August von Kotzebue who was suspected of being an agent of Czar Alexander I.

167. *Pyotr Kozlov*

Pyotr Kuzmich Kozlov was born on 15th October 1863 in Smolensk, Russia, and he died on 26th September 1935 (aged 72 years) in Petergof, Russia. A traveller and explorer who studied Mongolia and Tibet, Pyotr joined the expedition of Nikolai Przhevalsky. After his death, he continued his travelling in Asia and explored and described the upper reaches of the Yellow River, Yangtse and Mekong Rivers. He also explored the Gobi desert and discovered the ruins of Khara-Khoto, a city destroyed by the Ming Dynasty of China. It took him many years to excavate the site and he uncovered many books.

Do you know: Pyotr's discovered a number of royal burials. He bought back the samples of 2000-year-old textiles.

168. *Adam Johann von Krusenstern*

Adam Johann von Krusenstern was born on 10th October 1770 in Hagudi, Rapla Parish, Estonia, and he died on 12th August 1846 (aged 75 years) in Tallinn, Estonia. Adam was a Russian admiral and explorer who led the first Russian circumnavigation of the globe. The main reason for this expedition was the development of the fur trade with Alaska and to establish trade with China and Japan. They also wanted to examine the coast of California to establish if they could set up a colony there. Detailed maps and recordings were made for the entire voyage which was published, including an atlas. His work on counteracting the effects of iron on the compass was adopted by the navy.

Do you know: The Russians named two ships and a crater from the Moon after him.

169. Alexander Gordon Laing

Major Alexander Gordon Laing was born on 27th December 1794 in Edinburgh, USA, and he died on 26th September 1826 (aged 31 years) in Araouane, Mali. A British officer, Alexander was the first European to reach Timbuktu from the North and also find the source of River Rokel. He tried to locate the source of River Niger but was hindered by the natives. He was asked to travel to Mandingo Country with the aim of abolishing slave trade and to open new opportunities for commerce. He undertook the journey to Timbuktu across the desert of Tanezrouft.

Do you know: On his journey to Timbuktu, Alexander was looted, plundered and had his right hand cut off and never made it back from there.

170. Richard Lander

Richard Lemon Lander was born on 8th February 1804 in Truro, United Kingdom, and he died on 6th February 1834 (aged 30 years) in Nigeria. Richard was an explorer of western Africa. Upon Clapperton's death Richard took over the expedition as he was the only European member of the team. They followed it for 160 km and reached the delta. His third expedition to Africa was as the leader of an expedition with the aim of making a settlement for trade at the junction of Niger and Benue Rivers. This expedition was faced with a lot of difficulties. Richard himself was attacked and later died of his injuries.

Do you know: Richard Lemon Lander, in 1835, was the first winner of the Royal Geographical Society Founder's Medal which was given away to determine the course and termination of River Niger.

171. Grigory Langsdorff

Grigory Langsdorff was born on 8th April 1774 in Wollstein, Germany, and he died on 9th June 1852 (aged 77 years) in Freiburg im Breisgau, Germany. A naturalist and physician, Grigory was a part of the Russian team that circumnavigated the Earth. While posted in Brazil he collected many specimens of plants, animals and minerals and explored the flora and fauna of the area. Grigory led an ambitious expedition from Sao Paulo to Para in the Amazon and invited a host of other scientists and artists for the exploration, illustration and documentation of that expedition. These records were not published and were lost in the archives for about a century.

Do you know: During expedition Grigory was inflicted with a disease and went insane.

172. Jean-Francois de Galaup

Jean-Francois de Galaup was born on 23rd August 1741 in Albi, France, and he died in 1788 (aged 47 years) in the Solomon Islands. A French naval officer noted for his expedition to the Oceania to complete the discoveries of James Cook in the Pacific area, Jean-Francois intended to correct and complete the maps of the area while trying to establish trade and open new routes. They were to explore both the North and the South Pacific. He touched upon Alaska, East Asia, Japan, Russia, South Pacific and Australia. He sent the news of reaching France soon and sent his journals and charts back to France but he was never heard again.

Do you know: Jean-Francois was also the first European to reach the island of Maui near the present day Hawaiin Islands.

173. Albert von Le Coq

Albert von Le Coq was born on 8th September 1860 in Berlin, Germany, and he died on 21st April 1930 (aged 70 years) in Berlin, Germany. Albert was a brewery owner and wine merchant who got interested in archaeology later in life. He became a famous explorer of Central Asia. He planned and organized expeditions into Asia, especially near the Silk Route. Albert was chosen to lead one of these expeditions on which they found a network of Buddhist cave temples in China. They claimed to have discovered a Manichaean library but most of the manuscripts were destroyed during the excavations.

Do you know: All the artifacts that were excavated were put on display in the museum in Germany and were destroyed when the British bombed it during World War II.

174. John Ledyard

John Ledyard was born in November 1751, Connecticut, USA, and he died on 10th January 1789 (aged 37 years) in Cairo, Egypt. John was an American explorer who joined Captain Cook on his final voyage and covered the Cape of Good Hope to Tonga, Tahiti, Alaska, Hawaii and Kamchatka. John also took on a bold expedition of exploring the American continent. His next venture was an expedition from the Red Sea to the Atlantic. While in Cairo, John Ledyard accidentally poisoned himself and died.

Do you know: John's book was the first work to be protected by Copyright in the United States and is in Rare book Bibliographies as the first travelogue with a description of Hawaii ever to be published in America.

175. Ludwig Leichhardt

Ludwig Leichhardt was born on 23rd October 1813 in Tauche, Germany, and he disappeared on 3rd April 1848 (aged 34 years) in Darling Downs, Australia. Ludwig was a Prussian explorer and naturalist who was known for his exploration of northern and central Australia. He first came to Australia to explore inland Australia. He went to Hunter valley to study the geology, flora, fauna and the farming techniques of that region, collecting specimens to take with him. His first expedition from Moreton Bay to Port Essington was a 4800-km journey overland. He next explored the Condamine River and southern Queensland.

Do you know: Friedrich Wilhelm Ludwig was awarded the annual prize of Paris Geographical Society as well as the Patron's Medal for the most important discovery.

176. Jacob Le Maire

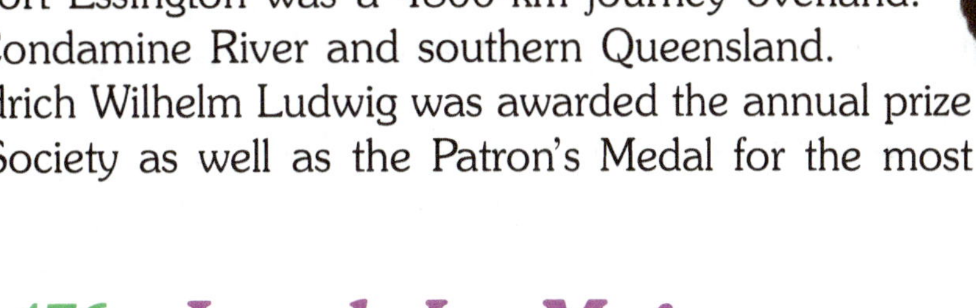

Jacob Le Maire was born in about 1585 in Antwerp, Belgium, and he died on 22nd December 1616 (aged 31 years) Indian Ocean. Jacob was a Dutch explorer who is famous for circumnavigating the Earth twice in 1615 and 1616. Jacob and Willem Schouten sailed across the Pacific visiting the Polynesian Islands. They were the first Europeans to visit the Tonga Islands; they sailed along New Ireland and visited the adjacent islands, which came to be known as Schouten Islands, and moved onto Java completing the circumnavigation. Jacob died on his way sailing back home after release.

Do you know: The Strait between Tierra del Fuego and Isla de los Estados was named the Le Maire Strait in his honour.

177. Alexey Leonov

Alexey Arkhipovich Leonov was born on 30th May 1934   in the Listvyanka, West Siberian Krai, USSR, and he is now retired. A Russian cosmonaut, Alexey was the first human to exit a spacecraft for a 12-minute space walk. He was tied to the spacecraft by a 5.35-metre tether. Alexey commanded the Soviet half of the Apollo-Soyuz mission which was the first joint space mission between the Soviet Union and the United States. Alexey is an accomplished artist and his artistic work has been published. He took coloured pencils and paper into space where he sketched the Earth and drew the portraits of the Apollo crew.

Do you know: Alexey's spacesuit had inflated in the vacuum of space so much that he could not re-enter the capsule and was barely able to get back inside.

178. David Livingstone

David Livingstone was born on 19th March 1813 in Blantyre, United Kingdom, and he died on 1st May 1873 (aged 59 years) in Zambia. A Scottish missionary, David was passionate about exploring Africa and finding the source of River Nile. He worked relentlessly on his exploration. He went to Africa to explore, map and navigate the rivers which would open up Africa to the traders and missionaries thus promoting Evangelism. He mapped the entire course of the Zambezi River and was the first European to see the Mosi-oa-Tunya waterfall which he renamed Victoria Falls.

Do you know: David Livingstone worked towards the abolition of slave trade, initiated education and health care for the Africans.

179. Louis-Philippe Loncke

Louis-Philippe Loncke was born on 3rd March 1977 in Mouscron, Belgium and he still lives today. A motivational speaker and adventurer, Louis-Philippe crossed the Simpson desert on foot in 2008, crossed the Tasmanian Wilderness, traversed Iceland and toured the Belgian waters in a kayak. His first solo adventure was the crossing of the Tasmanian Wilderness which brought him recognition in Australia. After crossing Simpson desert he went on to traverse Iceland in summers and toured the Belgian waters in a kayak.

Do you know: Louis-Philippe Loncke started the Chocolate-Sherpa expedition where he walked 400 km from Kathmandu to Everest base camp distributing chocolate.

180. Douglas Mawson

Douglas Mawson was born on 5th May 1882 in Shipley, US, and he died on 14th October 1958 (aged 76 years) in Brighton, Australia. A geologist and academic, Douglas led an expedition to the Antarctic sector south of Australia which was mostly unexplored with the aim to carry out scientific studies. They mapped the coastline and took geological samples. On their return they defined the exact location of the South Pole. Later, he also led a joint research expedition which resulted in the formation of the Australian Antarctic Territory.

Do you know: During the expedition Douglas barely made it back to the camp. Two of his three teammates fell into a crevasse along with most of their supplies and sled-dogs. And the other teammate died due to a disease which came about because he had to eat dog-meat to survive.

181. Nain Singh Rawat

Nain Singh Rawat was born on 21st October 1830 in Kumaon, India, and he died on 1st February 1882 (aged 52 years) in Moradabad, India. Nain Singh was an Indian explorer who explored the Himalayan region for the British. His first exploration was with the Germans where he travelled to Lake Mansarovar and Rakas Tal and on to Ladakh. He was trained under the British and was sent to be a spy-explorer. During these explorations Nain Singh mapped the trade route from Nepal to Tibet. He was the first person to determine the altitude and the exact location of Lhasa. He also travelled along the Tsangpo, a major Tibetan River and mapped most of its course.

Do you know: Nain Singh Rawat was a spy-explorer for the British and had to move around in the disguises of monks or traders to avoid suspicion.

182. Charles Albanel

Charles Albanel was born in 1616 in Ardes, France, and he died on 11 January 1696 (aged 80 years) in Sault Ste. Marie, Canada. A French missionary who explored Canada, Charles spent many winters with Montagnais Indians and learnt about their customs. He led a party that went by Saguenay River and may have been the first European to reach Hudson Bay. He took on other expeditions to explore the then unknown area. After returning in 1688 to Canada, he served at missions in Western Canada and died at Sault Ste. Marie. Lake Albanel, which runs parallel is named after him.

Do you know: Charles Albanel was captured by the English and taken to England where he convinced his captor to send him back to France.

183. William Adams

William Adams was born on 24th September 1564 in Gillingham, United Kingdom, and he died on 16th May 1620 (aged 56 years) in Hirado, Nagasaki Prefecture, Japan. William Adams was an English navigator who was the first person of his nationality to reach Japan. He was one of the few survivors of the five ship expeditions. He settled there and decided to take on Japanese culture and became the first ever Samurai of western origin. He directed the construction of western style ships in the country and was helpful in establishing trade with the Netherlands and England and establishing trading factories in Japan.

Do you know: The character of John Blackthorne in the best-selling novel, Shogun, was based on William Adams.

184. *Afonso de Albuquerque*

Afonso de Albuquerque was born in 1453 in the Alhandra, near Lisbon, Portugal, and he died on 16th December 1515 (aged 62 years) at sea, off Goa, India. Afonso was a Portuguese General and the first duke of Goa, India. He was the first European in Renaissance to raid the Persian Gulf. He led the first voyage by a European fleet into the Red Sea. He was considered instrumental in building and securing the Portuguese Empire in the Orient, the Middle East and Oceania. Afonso de Albuquerque closed all the naval passages of the Indian Ocean to the Atlantic, making it a Portuguese monopoly. He is credited with the conquest of Goa and the Malacca.

Do you know: Afonso de Albuquerque has a record of defeating large armies and fleets capturing the Ormuz against the Persians with a fleet of only seven ships.

185. *John Rae*

John Rae was born on 30th September 1813 in Orkney, Scotland, and he died on 22nd July 1893 (aged 80 years) in London, England. John Rae was a Scottish surgeon and Arctic explorer who is best known for the exploration of parts of Canada. He found the final portion of the Northwest Passage and the Rae Strait is named after him. John Rae was renowned for his skill as a hunter and excellent boat handling. He could live off the land and travel long distances for which he had great stamina. He made three journeys along the Arctic coast. During these expeditions they explored Mackenzie River, Victoria Island and the south coast of Victoria Island.

Do you know: John Rae was never given the recognition for discovering the Northwest Passage when he was alive.

186. *Knud Rasmussen*

Knud Johan Victor Rasmussen was born on 7th June 1879 in Greenland, and he died on 21st December 1933 (aged 54 years) in Copenhagen, Denmark. An anthropologist, Knud was the first European to cross the Northwest Passage on a dog-sled and mapped the North Coast of Greenland. He took on a journey of 1,000 km across inland ice to negate Peary's claim that a channel divided Pearyland from Greenland. He was awarded an Honorary Fellowship from the American Geographical Society in 1912, and its Daly Medal in 1924. Knud Johan was made honorary doctor at the University of Copenhagen in 1924.

Do you know: Knud Rasmussen's biggest project was to find the origin of the Eskimo race for which he collected ethnographic, archaeological and biological data.

187. Laszlo Almasy

Laszlo Almasy was born on 22nd August 1895 in Austria-Hungary, and he died on 22nd March 1951 (aged 55 years) in Salzburg, Austria. A Hungarian aristocrat, motorist and aviator, Laszlo planned the first exploration of the Libyan Desert by airplane with Count Zichy. His next plan was to find the Zerzura, the Oasis of birds. This expedition used both cars and a moth airplane. The attempt to reach the valley by car failed but Sir Robert flying the plane discovered a green valley they assumed was one of the three lost valleys of the Zerzura. In the next expedition to find Zerzura they entered the valley and confirmed it as the third valley of Zerzura.

Do you know: In the Oscar winning movie 'The English Patient', the character and events describe the expeditions of Laszlo Almasy into the Libyan Desert.

188. Matteo Ricci

Matteo Ricci was born on 6th October 1552 in the Macerata, Italy, and he died on 11th May 1610 (aged 58 years) in Beijing, China. A Jesuit Priest, Matteo was the first European to enter the Forbidden City and was wanted for his services in astronomy and calendrial science. His accurate predictions of Solar eclipses were valued as they were considered significant in the Chinese culture. He managed to convert several Chinese officials to Catholicism. Matteo Ricci composed the first western style map of the world in Chinese which is now known as 'Impossible Black Tulip' because of its rarity.

Do you know: Matteo Ricci and his mate Ruggieri also compiled the first ever Portuguese-to-Chinese dictionary, the first in any European language.

189. Charles John Andersson

Charles John Andersson was born on 4th March 1827 in Varmland, Sweden, and he died on 9th July 1867 (aged 40 years) in Angola. Charles was a adventurer, trader, explorer and collector of natural history specimens and hunter noted for the exploration of southern Africa in the present day Namibia which was largely unexplored at that time, Charles explored Lake Ngami and Okavango River. He wrote the account of his travels in books which he could never get published due to the lack of funds. He had repeated financial problems. Even though his main interests were exploration and natural history, he often needed to earn money through trade and hunting.

Do you know: Charles John Andersson continued exploring towards Angola despite being seriously ill to establish a trading route to Europe and died on his way back.

190. *Ingolfur Arnarson*

Ingolfur Arnarson was born on around in 844 (59), Rivedal, Sunnfjord, Sogn og Fjordane, Norge and died on 903 (51-67) in Reykjavik, Island. Considered one of the first Nordic settlers in Iceland, Ingolfur gave the name Reykjavik to the area in 874. He had to leave Norway because of getting into a feud and decided to settle on the island that others had found in the Atlantic. The Irish slaves killed his brother and Ingolfur hunted them down on an island and killed them. The Irishmen were then known as Vestmannaeyjar (Westman Islands). That's how the island got its name.

Do you know: Ingolfur Arnarson threw his chieftain's seat pillars into the sea and decided to settle where they came ashore. It took three years to find them in a small bay.

191. *Jacob Roggeveen*

Jacob Roggeveen was born on 1st February 1659 in Middleburg, Netherlands, and he died on 31st January 1729 (aged 69 years) in Middleburg, Netherlands. A Dutch explorer Jacob was sent to find Australia to open a western trade route but instead he landed on Easter Island and he called it so because he landed there on Easter Day. He also mapped two islands in Society Islands and six new Islands in the Tuamotu Archipelago. Jacob Roggeveen moved ahead to Samoa where he chartered four more Islands.

Do you know: Jacob Roggeveen was arrested for violating the monopoly of VOC and his ships were confiscated. After a lengthy law suit he was finally compensated for his losses and they paid his crew.

192. *Vladimir Atlasov*

Vladimir Vasilyevich Atlasov or Otlasov was born in 1661 in Veliky Ustyug, Russia, and he died in 1711. Known for organizing the first systematic exploration of Kamchatka Penninsula, and the volcanic Island of Atlasov which was named after him, Vladimir led an expedition to the Kamchatka and travelled on a reindeer with about 120 men. During this expedition he met the natives tribes. He made alliances with some of them and fought against others killing many of their people. He was sent back to be an administrator of the Kamchatka. His methods were so brutal that his men made a complaint against him and imprisoned him. He was later killed by a band of mutineers.

Do you know: In Kamchatka, Vladimir chased and killed 150 men to get back the reindeer they had stolen.

193. *Voin Rimsky Korsakov*

Voin Andreyevich Rimsky Korsakov was born on 14th July 1822 in Oryol Oblast, Russia, and he died on 4th November 1871 (aged 49 years) Pisa, Italy. Voin Rimsky was a Russian naval officer and captain of the Vostok. In the 1850s and 1860s, he researched the area of the Sea of Japan near Ussuri Krai. Later, a small archipelago was named after him. He was the brother of the famous composer Nikolai Rimsky Korsakov, and the former Ainu village of Kushunkotan on Sakhalin is today named Korsakov.

Do you know: Voin Rimsky Korsakov graduated from the School for Mathematical and Navigational Sciences in Saint Petersburg. He served as a naval officer and commander of the schooner Vostok in the flotilla under the administration of Admiral Yevfimy Putyatin.

194. *Willem Janszoon Blaeu*

Willem Janszoon Blaeu was born in 1571, Seventeen Provinces, and he died on 21st October 1638 (aged 67 years) in Amsterdam, Netherlands. Willem Janszoon Blaeu was a Dutch cartographer. He was the founder of a large publishing firm that became famous in the field of cartography under the name Blaeu. The first maps of Blaeu appeared in 1604. Later, he also started printing wall charts and large atlases. He invented mechanical devices for improving the technics of printing.

Do you know: As an astronomer, Willem Janszoon Blaeu made careful observations of a moon eclipse; he discovered a variable star now known as P Cygni, and carried out a measurement of a degree on the surface of the earth.

195. *Candido Rondon*

Candido Mariano da Silva Rondon was born on 5th May 1865 in Brazil, and he died on 19th January 1958 (aged 92 years) in Rio de Janeiro, Brazil. A Brazilian military officer, he became famous for his exploration of Mato Grosso and the western Amazon Basin. He explored Mato Grosso extensively as he had to lay the telegraph line as an army engineer. Candido laid about 4,000 miles of telegraph lines through the thick forests of Brazil. During the course of laying telegraph lines towards the Amazon he discovered River Juruena and also the Nambikwara tribe.

Do you know: Candido Rondon accompanied Theodore Roosevelt in exploring the River of Doubt, which was renamed Rio Roosevelt.

196. *Henry Russell*

Henry Russell or Henry Patrick Marie was born in 1834 in Toulouse, France, and he died in 5th February 1909 (aged 75 years) in Biarritz, France. Henry was known for the Pyrenean exploration of which he was one of the pioneers. His first expedition was to North America at the age of 23 where he climbed Pic de Neouvielle and Ardiden and the Monte Perdido, thrice. His next voyage lasted three years when he travelled to Russia, Beijing, crossed the Gobi Desert twice. He stayed in Shanghai and Hong Kong and then travelled to Australia and New Zealand. He went to India and Cairo before going back to France.

Do you know: Henry Russell climbed the Vignemale thirty-three times and hosted lavish banquets at the caves he had made there.

197. *Heinrich Barth*

Heinrich Barth was born on 16th February 1821 in Hamburg, Germany, and he died on 25th November 1865 (aged 44 years) in Berlin, Germany. Heinrich was a German scholar and explorer of Africa. His first expedition was under an explorer of the Sahara, James Richardson. After his death Heinrich carried on the expedition all alone. He was the first European to visit Adamawa. He covered 12,000 miles on this expedition. He studied the topography, history, civilization and languages of the countries he visited. He went on to become a famous historian of Africa as he paid attention to the culture and the people rather than the commercial exploitation of the region.

Do you know: Heinrich's accounts of his travels are considered invaluable and are still used by the historians of Africa.

198. *Henry Walter Bates*

Henry Walter Bates was born on 8th February 1825 in Leicester, England, and he died on 16th February 1892 (aged 67 years) in London. Henry Walter Bates was an English naturalist and explorer. He explored the Amazon Rainforests and the Amazon Basin along with his friend Alfred Wallace. They reached Para, Brazil to collect specimen to gather facts towards solving the problem of the 'origin of species' as stated by them in a letter. Their aim was to send the specimen back home where an agent would sell them. He collected about 14,712 species of insects of which at least 8,000 were unknown. He was the first person to give the scientific account of mimicry in animals which is named after him and called Batesian mimicry.

Do you know: Henry stayed in the Amazon basin region for 11 years.

199. *George Bass*

George Bass was born on 30th January 1771 in Aswarby, United Kingdom, and he died on 5th February 1803 (aged 32 years) at sea. George Bass was a naval surgeon and explorer of Australia. He joined the Royal navy as a surgeon but his interest in navigation was noticed and he was transferred to another ship which was headed to Australia. On landing he with two others explored the George's River and Botany Bay and suggested that a settlement be made there. He also studied the flora and fauna of the region. He discovered a Strait in the Tasmanian region which was named after him.

Do you know: George Bass sailed with a cargo ship going to South America and was never heard again.

200. *Lafayette Bunnell*

Lafayette Houghton Bunnell was born on 13th March 1824 in Rochester, New York, USA, and he died on 21st July 1903 (aged 79 years) in Homer, Minnesota, USA. Lafayette Houghton Bunnell was an American physician, writer and explorer. He is noted for exploring the Yosemite Valley. Lafayette was a member of the Mariposa Battalion which in search for the Native American Tribal leaders discovered the Yosemite Valley and named many of its features. He went on to write an account of his exploration and the actions of his battalion. The major source of knowledge about the Ahwahnechee, the indigenous people who lived in the Yosemite Valley, is through his writings.

Do you know: Lafayette Houghton Bunnell settled down in Minnesota and wrote the histories of the upper Mississippi.

201. *James Clark Ross*

Captain Sir James Clark Ross was born on 15th April 1800 in London, UK, and he died on 3rd April 1862 (aged 62 years) in Aston Abbotts, UK. A British naval officer known for his exploration of the Arctic and the Antarctic, James located the North Magnetic Pole and undertook an expedition to the Antarctic to look for the South Magnetic Pole. While on this expedition he discovered the Ross Sea, Victoria Land and mapped the coast of Graham Land. He was knighted upon his return to England. His closest friend was Crozier, with whom he sailed many times. He also lived in the Ancient House of the Abbots of Saint Albans in Buckinghamshire.

Do you know: James Clark Ross discovered two volcanoes on his Antarctic expedition and called them Mount Terror and Mount Erebus after the two ships of the expedition.

202. *Anatoly Sagalevich*

Anatoly Mikhailovich Sagalevich was born on 5th September 1938 in Russia and he still lives today. Anatoly is a Russian explorer who was the pilot of MIR-1DSV (Deep Submergence Vehicles) that reached the seabed at the North Pole during an expedition Arktika. He has been the director of the Russian Deepwater Submersibles Laboratory. He was a part of the construction of Pisces VIII and IX DSVs and has completed more than 300 submersions as the chief pilot of DSV's. He led more than 28 expeditions in DSVs and found the wrecks of the Titanic and the Bismarc. Anatoly has been awarded the 'Hero of the Russian Federation' for courage and heroism shown in extreme conditions.

Do you know: Anatoly Sagalevich holds the record for the deepest freshwater dive at 5,371 ft in Lake Baikal.

203. *Martin Alonso Pinzon*

Martin Alonso Pinzon was born in 1441 in Palos de la Frontera, Spain, and he died on 31st March 1493 (aged 52 years) in La Rabida Friary, Spain. A Spanish mariner, shipbuilder, navigator and explorer, Martin captained the Pinta on Christopher Columbus' first voyage to America. Martin's suggestion to change course brought the fleet to landfall in the Bahamas on 12th October 1492. Against orders, he left the fleet near Cuba to search for gold and spices by himself. Martin's ship again separated from Columbus on the return voyage, but this time did not try to reconnect with the rest of Columbus' fleet.

Do you know: Despite the brother's effort, Columbus beat Martin's home, immortalizing Martin Pinzon in history for his disloyalty.

204. *Diogo Cao*

Diogo Cao was born about 1450 in Vila Real, Portugal and he died about 1486. A navigator, Diogo was an important explorer in the Age of Discovery. He was the one who discovered the mouth and estuary of the Congo River when he was sent by the Portuguese King to explore the African Coast. He explored on further down to Angola and marked a second pillar. He took a second voyage to Africa. When King John II of Portugal restarted the work of Henry the Navigator, he sent out Cao to open up the African coast still further beyond the equator.

Do you know: Diogo Cao is said to have died near Cape Cross by one report and by another he is said to have returned to Portugal.

205. *Hermenegildo Capelo*

Hermenegildo de Brito Capelo was born in 4th February 1841 in Palmela, Portugal, and he died in 4th May 1917 (aged 75 years) in Lisbon, Portugal. Hermenegildo was an officer of the Portuguese navy and an explorer who is best known for mapping the area between Angola and Mozambique. He along with Roberto Ivens was the first European to cross the Central Africa from coast to coast between Angola and Mozambique. They also mapped the commercial route between Angola and Mozambique. Their achievements were recorded in a two-volume book. The King of Portugal received them triumphantly on their return home from this expedition.

Do you know: Hermenegildo de Brito Capelo was Vice-Admiral until he was exiled; it ended his military career.

206. *Gadiel Sanchez Rivera*

Gadiel 'Cho' Sanchez Rivera was born on 13th October 1978 in Pucallpa, Peru, and he still lives today. Gadiel is a Peruvian adventurer and a jungle expert. He was hired by the English explorer Ed Stafford as a guide for the journey on the Amazon but later made him an assistant and Gadiel finished this walk for him for two years. In 2013, he circumnavigated Lake Titicaca by kayak with Philippe Loncke. During this expedition they took the underwater photos of the Bolivian coasts trying to find the living habitat of the Giant Frog Species. He was also the guide and consultant to the Polish explorer Marcin Gienieczko.

Do you know: Gadiel Sanchez Rivera quit an industrial logging job because it was very unpleasant to cut down trees and spoil the natural environment.

207. *Svetlana Savitskaya*

Svetlana Yevgenyevna Savitskaya was born on 8th August 1948 in Moscow and she still lives today in Soviet Union, and is now retired. Svetlana was a Russian cosmonaut who had the honour of being the first woman to do a spacewalk and the second woman in space. She flew to space as a part of the Soyuz T-7 mission with two other cosmonauts. During this flight she moved outside the spacecraft and cut and welded metals in space along with a colleague. After her return, she was made the commander of the all-female Soyuz crew in commemoration of International Woman's Day, a mission that was later cancelled.

Do you know: Svetlana Savitskaya set 18 world records on MIG aircraft and three records in team parachute jumping.

208. *Joao de Castro*

Joao de Castro was born on 27th February 1500 in Lisbon, Portugal, and he died on 6th June 1548 (aged 48 years) in Goa, India. Joao was a Portuguese nobleman and naval officer who contributed to the science of navigation. He was also the first person to note that the compass needle deviated due to the magnetic effects. Joao spent 20 years in Africa where he was a part of the Seige of Tunis for which he was rewarded. But he refused both the knighthood and the rewards. He sailed for India afterwards. On landing in Goa he helped the Portuguese in the release of Fort Diu. After his return to Goa he served as the Fourth Viceroy of Portuguese India.

Do you know: Joao wrote three Pilot books which are considered remarkable for their scientific observations and contributed majorly to the study of seafaring.

209. **Thomas Cavendish**

Thomas Cavendish was born on 19th September 1560 in the Trimley Saint Martin, United Kingdom, and he died in May 1592 (aged 32 years) in the Atlantic Ocean, sailing on the Atlantic Ocean. An English navigator and privateer, Thomas was the leader of the third circumnavigation of the world and discovered Port Desire, now in Argentina. Knighted by Queen Elizabeth I on his return, Thomas tried to take a second American-Pacific expedition but his fleet could not sail through the Strait of Magellan and he died trying to get back to England at the age of 32.

Do you know: Thomas Cavendish inherited a fortune at the age of 12 from his father's estate.

210. *John Lloyd Stephens*

John Lloyd Stephens was born on 28th November 1805, New Jersey, United States, and he died on 13th October 1852 (aged 47 years) in New York, US. An American diplomat and writer, John is best known for the rediscovery of the Mayan civilization and the planning of the Panama railroad. He visited many archaeological sites in Eastern Europe and the Middle East and decided to locate the ruins in Central America.This discovery generated a lot of scholarly interest and public excitement. They made a second expedition to 44 different ancient sites. He was recommended for the post of Minister to the Netherlands but Martin Van Buren nominated Harmanus Bleecker.

Do you know: John Lloyd Stephens was the President of the Panama railroad Company which planned the laying of the railroads.

211. *Jean Chardin*

Jean Baptiste Chardin was born on 16th November 1643 in Paris, France, and he died on 5th January 1713 (aged 69 years) in Chiswick, London, United Kingdom. A French jeweller and traveller, Jean Chardin wrote a 10-volume book on Persia where he lived for four years and learnt the language, customs and traditions. He made short journeys to India, the Caspian and the Persian gulf. His written accounts are acknowledged as being of value and the best description of Islamic nations. He visited India and returned to Persia in 1669. The next year he arrived in Paris.

Do you know: Jean Baptiste Chardin was the official agent of jewels for the Shah of Persia as well as the court jeweller of England.

212. *Otto Schmidt*

Otto Yulyevich Schmidt was born on 30th September 1891 in Mogilev, Belarus, and he died on 7th September 1956 (aged 65 years) in Mozzhinka, Russia. Otto Yulyevich Schmidt was a mathematician, scientist, astronomer and Arctic explorer. He led expeditions to the Arctic in which he established the first scientific research station and explored the Kara Sea and the west coast of Severnaya Zemlya. He made another voyage there which was a non-stop journey from Arkhangelsk to the Pacific Ocean without stopping for winters. It was done for the first time in history. The authorities awarded Otto Schmidt three Orders of Lenin, three other orders and many medals.

Do you know: Otto Yulyevich Schmidt is responsible for developing the higher education system in the Soviet Union.

213. *Aleksei Chirikov*

Aleksei Ilyich Chirikov was born on 24 December 1703 in the Russian Empire and he died on November 1748 (aged 45 years) in Moscow, Russia. A Russian explorer Aleksei who along with Vitus Bering was the first Russian to reach the North-west coast of North America. He was the second-in-command on the Kamchatka expeditions where he assisted Vitus Bering in mapping Siberia's Arctic coast and explored routes to America, discovering the Prince of Wales Island in Alaska. He took part in creating the final map of the Russian discoveries in the Pacific Ocean.

Do you know: Aleksei Chirikov has been honoured by his name being given to two Capes, an underwater mountain in the Pacific Ocean and an Island.

214. *Vasily Chichagov*

Vasily Yakovlevich Chichagov was born on 28th February 1726 in the Russian Empire and he died on 4th April 1809 (aged 83 years) in Saint Petersburg in Russia. A Russian Navy Admiral and explorer, Vasily was in charge of the expedition to find the Northwest Passage between the Atlantic and Pacific Oceans along the Siberian coast. He was a successful naval leader and was a part of the Russo-Turkish war against the Ottomans. During the Russo-Swedish war he was commander-in-chief of the Baltic Fleet and he won some important battles which allowed the war to come to an end.

Do you know: Vasily Chichagov was very attached to Great Britain as he was educated there; he married an English woman and settled in the United Kingdom.

215. *Fletcher Christian*

Fletcher Christian was born on 25th September 1764 in Eaglesfield, Cumbria, United Kingdom and he died on 20th September 1793 (aged 29 years) on the Pitcairn Islands. Fletcher was a sailor by profession. After a career in the Royal Navy he was sailing with William Bligh on a 2-year voyage from Tahiti to the West Indies. During the Mutiny he tried to establish a settlement and build a colony in Tubuai. On reaching Tahiti he married a local woman and moved on to the Pitcairn Islands.

Do you know: Fletcher Christian's sons said to be the ancestors of almost all the people with the surname of Christian on Pitcairn and Norfolk Islands.

216. *Boris Chukhnovsky*

Boris Grigoryevich Chukhnovsky was born on 28 April 1898 in Saint Petersburg, Soviet Union, and he died on 30th September 1975 (aged 77 years). A pilot and Arctic explorer, Boris was one of the pioneers of Soviet Arctic aviation. He flew many flights in the Arctic region taking the aerial pictures of Novaya Zemlya. He was a coordinator of the team to rescue Airship Italia expedition returning from the North Pole where he himself was stranded while trying to find the team but gave their rescue a priority.

Do you know: Boris Chukhnovsky participated in the creation of the Arctic Aviation Service and developed a flying boat which could work in the Arctic.

217. *Hugh Clapperton*

Bain Hugh Clapperton was born on 18th May 1788 in Annan, Scotland, United Kingdom, and he died on 13th April 1827 (aged 39 years) in Sokoto, Nigeria. A Scottish naval officer, Hugh was the first European who went to West Africa giving the first account of the area now known as northern Nigeria. He also became the first European to see Lake Chad and to enter a Sudanese province. He travelled to Kano, Katsina, Sokoto and Zaria, now all in Nigeria.

Do you know: Hugh Clapperton reached Sokoto intending to continue but due to the breaking out of a war he was not allowed to leave. He was detained and after many months of suffering from malaria, dysentery and depression he died there.

218. *Nicolau Coelho*

Nicolau Coelho was born about 1460 in Portugal and he died in 1502 in Mozambique. Nicolau was a Portuguese navigator and explorer who participated in the voyage of the discovery of the route to India with Vasco da Gama. He was commanding the ship 'Berrio' which was the first to return. It was his ship that was also the first to reach Mozambique and make contact with the Sultan of Quiloa. He was also the captain of the ship in a fleet of thirteen which made the discovery of Brazil under Pedro Alvares Cabral. They sailed to Mozambique, Kenya, Tanzania and finally reached India.

Do you know: Nicolau Coelho, on his return from the discovery of the route, was given a generous pension, lands and a new coat of arms. He was also made the Knight of the Royal House.

219. *Frank Cole*

Frank Cole was born in 1954 in Saskatchewan, Canada, and he died in 2000 (aged 46 years) in Mali, West Africa. Frank was a Canadian film-maker and a surfer. He is famous for being the first North American to cross the Sahara desert alone on a camel's back from the Atlantic Ocean to the Red Sea. This journey earned Frank a place in the Guinness Book of World Records. He made a documentary on his experiences called 'Life Without Death' which won him several awards. He grew up in different countries including Pakistan, Afghanistan, Czechoslovakia, Switzerland and South Africa. He could speak many languages.

Do you know: Frank Cole was murdered by two bandits who stole his camera gear and film recordings when he tried to cross Sahara (Desert) the second time.

220. George Comer

Captain George Comer was born in April 1858 in Quebec, Canada, and he died in 1937 (aged 79 years) in East Haddam, Connecticut, USA. A well-known whaling captain and an authority on Hudson Bay Inuit, George was also a Polar explorer, cartographer, author and photographer. He made 14 Arctic and 3 Antarctic voyages during his lifetime. George Comer excavated Mount Dundas where he found the evidence of the Thule people who are the ancestors of the Inuits. George Comer was highly regarded for his Arctic anthropology, ethnology, natural history, geography and cartography work. Lacking formal training, George Comer was mentored by anthropologist Franz Boas.

Do you know: George Comer's first voyage to the Arctic was at the age of 17.

221. Frederick Cook

Frederick Albert Cook was born on 10th June 1865 in Callicoon, New York, United States, and he died on 5th August 1940 (aged 74 years) in New Rochelle, New York, United States. An American explorer, physician and ethnographer, Frederick became famous when he claimed to have reached the North Pole which gave rise to a controversy as the claim had already been made by Robert Peary. He laid claim to summiting the Denali Peak which also turned out to be fraudulent. He did make a discovery of the Meighen Island which was the only discovery in the American Arctic which was made by an American expedition. Frederick Cook was the surgeon on Robert Peary's 1891–92 Arctic Expedition, and on the Belgian Antarctic Expedition of 1897–99 led by Adrien de Gerlache. He contributed greatly to saving the lives of the crew when their ship (the Belgica) was ice-bound during the winter.

Do you know: Frederick Cook was charged with fraud for the claim to reach the North Pole and his Inuit companions stated that he had stopped much short of the Pole.